THE SPEAKING
VOICE

PRINCIPLES OF TRAINING
SIMPLIFIED AND CONDENSED

BY

KATHERINE JEWELL EVERTS

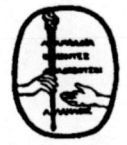

HARPER & BROTHERS
NEW YORK AND LONDON
MCMVIII

PREFACE

THIS little book on voice is the result of
its author's observation — first in the
college and social world, and later as reader,
teacher, and actress—of the crying need, in
each and all of these circles, for some simple
and practical instruction in the training of
the speaking voice.

There are volumes of recognized authority, considerable in length and exhaustive in
detail, which one who intends to use his voice
professionally should master, if possible, but
which it is almost impossible for the college,
society, or business man or woman to study
and follow, from sheer lack of time. This
book offers a method of voice training which
is the result of a deliberate effort to simplify
and condense, for general use, the principles
which are fundamental to all recognized sys-

iii

PREFACE

tems of vocal instruction. It contains practical directions accompanied by simple and fundamental exercises, first for the freeing of the voice and then for developing it when free.

Careful study of these directions and faithful practise of these exercises for fifteen minutes a day will do much toward converting our high-pitched, harsh, hard American instrument of torture into the low-toned, efficient agent of personality it was intended by nature to be.

To Dr. S. H. Clark of the University of Chicago, and to Dr. S. S. Curry of the School of Expression in Boston, I wish to express my gratitude for the inspiration to this task, which their books have given me. To Mr. George W. Ferguson of Berlin, and to Miss Caroline V. Smith of the State Normal School of Minnesota, I am deeply indebted for personal instruction in the training of my own instrument. My especial gratitude is due to my first teacher, Mrs. Lenora Austin Hamlin of Chicago, who, at a critical moment saved my voice for such work as it has had the

iv

PREFACE

honor to carry on, since my study with her;
and to my last teacher, Mr. J. W. Parson
Price, who has recently rescued it for further
efforts in the field of vocal interpretation.

KATHERINE JEWELL EVERTS.

PLAN OF THE BOOK

THE Voice throughout the book is treated
as an Instrument of Expression, with a
technique just as necessary to master as the
technique of the piano, violin, or any other
musical instrument. But before the study
of technique can be safely entered upon, the
instrument must be put in tune, so the work
falls naturally under three heads, and the
book is divided accordingly into three parts,
as follows:

vii

PLAN OF THE BOOK

INTRODUCTION

NEXT to that primary instinct, the instinct for self-preservation, the strongest impulse of the human heart is for self-expression.

The failure of society to provide simple and natural means of self-preservation has led to the American anarchist. The failure of education to provide for the training of the simple and natural means of self-expression has led to the American voice.

We cram the student's mind with a knowledge of beauty and truth, but do not free the channels of communication and expression through which, in the act of sharing the knowledge he has acquired, the student assimilates and recreates that beauty and truth and finds it a vital force in his soul life and a vital index of his culture.

world, a pure tone of the human voice, is a source of delight to the physiologist, but will only interfere with that feel for the free, full volume of sound which the student of voice as an instrument of thought and emotion is to make, as a first step in vocal training. Then, not as anatomists or physiologists, but as makers of music, let us look at, let us feel for, a tone.

I am "stung by the splendor of a sudden thought"; I desire to share it with you; the desire causes me to take a deep breath, a column of air rises, is converted into tone, passes into the mouth, and is moulded into the words which symbolize my thought. Let us, without further analysis, try this. Close your eyes, think of some line of prose or poetry which has moved you profoundly; let it take possession of you until you are seized by the desire to voice it. Still with closed eyes, feel yourself take the breath which is to be made into tone, and then into the words which stand for the thought. Hold that sensation, and study it with me for a moment. "But," you say, "the desire

to voice the thought does not seize me."
Very well, let me ask you a question. "Do
you like growing old?" Now your thought
was converted so swiftly into speech that
you had no time to study the conversion.
Once more, whether your answer be the
"Yes" of sixteen or the "No" of thirty,
close your eyes and feel for the tone you
are to use in making the single word Yes
or No.

Now, a little more in detail, let us see what
happens. · A thought full of emotion meets
the question, the desire to answer is born;
the need of breath to meet the desire con-
tracts the diaphragm (the pump); the chest
(the reservoir) fills; a column of air, pumped
and controlled by the diaphragm, and re-
enforced in the chest, rises, strikes the vocal cords (the "strings" of the instrument),
the strings vibrate, converting the air into
sound, into tone; the tone, re-enforced in all
the chambers of the head, passes into the
mouth, and is there moulded by the juxta-
position of the organs of speech (lips, teeth,
tongue) into the word, the single, monosyl-

labic word, Yes or No, which frames the thought. Now, once more, with closed eyes, sense the process and hold the sensation, but do not speak the word. Now, still once more, and this time, speak. Alas! did we say we were "makers of music"? Is this harmony, this harsh, hard, breathy, strident note? What is the trouble?

First of all, fundamental to all, and beyond a doubt the secret of the dissonance, you did not breathe before you spoke or as you spoke. I mean, really breathe. And that is the first point to be attacked. Breathe, breathe, breathe! you must learn how to breathe; you must get your pump, your diaphragm, into working order, you must master it, you must control it, you must not fetter it, you must give it a free chance to do its work. If you are a man, you have probably at least been fair in not tying down your pump; you have not encased yourself in steel bands and drawn them so tight that your diaphragm could not descend and perform its office. Yes, and if you are the athletic girl of to-day, you have probably learned the delight and

6

benefit of free muscular action. But you may still be suffering from the effect of your mother's crime in this direction. It may have sent you into the world with weakened muscles in control of the great pumping-station upon which must depend the beauty of your voice.

But whatever the condition or the cause, it must, if wrong, be made right. We must learn to breathe properly, freely, naturally. (Do not confuse "naturally" and "habitu-ally." In this connection these terms are op-posites rather than synonymes.) To breathe naturally we must do away with all con-striction. We must choose between the al-leged beauty of a disproportionately small waist and the charm of a beautiful and al-luring voice. We cannot have both. Then, off with tight corsets. Thank Heaven, they are the exception and not the rule to-day. Please note that I distinctly do not say, "Off with corsets," but only, "Off with ill-fitting corsets," for which "tight" is but another name. I believe, to digress a mo-ment, with our present method of dress, a

7

properly fitted corset is an absolute necessity, except in the rare instances where a perfectly proportioned and slender figure is also under the control of firm, well-trained muscles. In a first flush of rapture over the vision of the gentle ladies of Mr. Howells's Altruria, seen *Through the Eye of the Needle*, we feel that we can take a step toward that paradise by discarding the straitlaced tailored torture the present-day costume prescribes, for the corsetless grace of the Altrurian garment; but our enthusiasm is short-lived, as we realize that we are in modern America and must make as inconspicuously gracious an appearance as possible without violating the conventions. So, as I say, do not discard the corset, which is, for the majority of women, the saving grace of the present fashion in dress; only see that your corset brings out what is best in the figure God gave you, instead of disfiguring it, as undue constriction of any part of your body will inevitably do. Incidentally, by this precaution, save your voice as well.

But until we can be refitted, or readjust

8

the corsets we already wear, and the gowns made over them, we must avoid the discouraging effect of trying to work against the odds of a costume which interferes with our breathing, by making a practice of taking the breathing exercises involved in the first step, at night and in the morning. Five minutes of deep, free breathing from the diaphragm, lying flat on your back in bed at night and before you rise in the morning, will accomplish the desired result. The point in lying flat on your back is that in that position alone you can be sure you are breathing naturally, which is diaphragmatically. Indeed, you cannot, without great effort, and sometimes not even then, breathe any other way than naturally. I cannot tell you why. I can only say, try it and see.

Our first exercise, then, is to lie flat on the back at night and in the morning, when you are perfectly free, and, with closed eyes, take deep, long breaths, letting them go slowly, and studying the accompanying sensation until it is fixed fast and you feel you cannot lose it, but can reproduce, under any condition, the action which resulted in that sensation. The incidental effect of this exercise is to make one very sleepy. Indeed, nothing will so quickly and effectually put to flight that foe of the society woman and business man of to-day, insomnia, as the practice of deep, regular, natural breathing. Add counting each respiration, and it is an almost unfailing remedy. The only trouble for our purpose is that it is sometimes so swiftly soporific that we are asleep before the sensation is fixed fast and noted in consciousness: which is one object of the exercise. However, should we find the prescribed five minutes at night interfered with by coming drowsiness, we may yield in sleepy content, "sustained and soothed" by the thought that we shall be in splendid shape for the morning practice, with which nothing must interfere, "not headache, or sciatica, or leprosy, or thunder-stroke."

We are ready now for the third exercise. When, for five minutes in the morning, lying flat on your back, with closed eyes, you have taken deep, long breaths, letting them go slowly, yielding your whole body to the act of respiration, noting the effect and fixing fast the sensation, as a next step you are to stand up and repeat the operation. Still holding the sensation (not by tightening your muscles, or clenching your fists, or setting your teeth, but simply by thinking the sensation, letting it possess you), in this attitude of mind breathe naturally, standing instead of lying down. That is all. Don't be discouraged if the test prove unsatisfactory at first. Try an intermediate step. Sit on the side of your bed, or in a straight-back chair, and, closing your eyes and relaxing all your muscles except those governing the diaphragm, breathe. Now stand, well poised. By well poised, of course you know I mean with the weight perfectly balanced about the centre of gravity, which, in turn, means that a perpendicular dropped from the highest point of the lifted chest without encountering any part of your body, and especially not your abdomen (which should be held always back, so that it is flat, if not actually concave) will fall unobstructed to the floor, striking a point just between the balls of your feet. Standing thus, well poised, place the right hand on your body, just below your ribs at the base of the lungs, and your left hand on your back, just opposite your right hand; then breathe, and feel the diaphragm, as it descends, cause the torso, in turn, to expand from front to back, pressing against either hand. Let the breath go slowly, controlling its emission by controlling the diaphragm.

So the three exercises stand progressively thus:

First.—Breathe naturally, which is diaphragmatically, five minutes at night. (At first you can be sure of doing this only by lying flat on your back.)

Second.—Breathe naturally, which is diaphragmatically, for five minutes in the morning, and note the sensation.

Third.—Stand and test your newly acquired power by trying to breathe diaphragmatically while on your feet.

These three exercises constitute the first step in the first stage of vocal training, and that step is called "Learning to Support the Tone."

I know a little girl who, in the beginning of her career, alarmed her parents by refusing to utter a syllable or the semblance of a syllable until she was three years old, when she evidently considered herself ready for her maiden effort at speech. Prepared she proved, for, sitting at the window in her high chair one day, watching people pass, she remarked quietly and with perfect precision, "There goes Mrs. Tibbets." I find myself secretly wishing it were possible for you to refrain from speech, not for three years, but for three weeks, while you quietly prepare for speech by practising these three breathing exercises. It is quite the customary thing for the teacher of voice as an instrument of song to require of the student a period of silence—that is, a period in which only exercises are allowed, and songs, even the simplest, are forbidden. However, our only way to secure this condition would be to go into retreat; but, after all, one of the most encouraging things about this work is the remarkable effect upon the speaking voice of simply holding the thought of the right condition for tone, *thinking* the three exercises I have given you. It is not so remarkable, perhaps, in the light of the experiment recently made (I am told) in one of our great colleges, when three men daily performed a certain exercise, and three other men simply thought it intensely, and the resultant effect upon the muscles used in the act was marvellously similar. I am half afraid to have recalled this, lest you take advantage of the suggestion and relax your effort, or, out of curiosity, make the experiment. Please don't. I offer it only as an incentive to you, to *think* at least of the desired condition, if you cannot every day indulge in an active effort to attain it.

Please test at once the immediate effect of this third exercise. Take the attitude I have defined, and try once more any full-vowelled syllable. I think you will find the tone already improved.

II

LEARNING TO FREE THE TONE

WE have worked, so far, for support of
tone. We must now free the supported
tone, by freeing the channel for the emission
of the breath as it is converted into tone and
moulded into speech. We shall find that in
learning to support the tone we have gone
far toward securing that freedom; but the
habit of years is not easily overcome, and
every time you have spoken without proper
support of breath you have forced the tone
from the throat, by tightening the muscles
and closing the channel, thus making conditions which must now be reformed by steady,
patient effort. Yet it is not effort I want
from you now; it is lack of effort. It is
passivity; it is surrender. I want you to relax all the muscles which govern the organs

15

concerned in converting the breath into tone and moulding the tone into speech, all the muscles controlling the throat and mouth, including the lips and jaw. I want utter passivity of the parts from the point where the column of breath strikes the vocal cords to where, as tone, it is moulded into the word "No." Surrender to the desire to utter that word. Concentrate your thought on two things: the taking of the breath and the word it is to become. Now, lying down, or sitting easily, lazily, in a comfortable chair, or standing leaning against the wall, with closed eyes, surrender to the thought "No," and, taking a breath, speak. Still hard and unmusical you find? Yes, but I am sure not so hopelessly hard as before. What shall we do to relax the tense muscles, to release the throat and free the channel? At the risk of being written down a propagandist, in the ranks of the extreme dress-reformers, I shall say, first of all, take off those high, tight collars. Again, as with the corset, it is a case of a misfit rather than too tight a fit. If your collar is cut to fit, it need not be too high nor too tight for comfort, and it will still be becoming. You want it to cling to the neck and keep the line. Cut it to fit, and it will keep the line; then put in pieces of whalebone, if necessary, or resort to some of the many other devices now in vogue for keeping the soft collar erect, but don't choke yourself, either by fastening it too tight or cutting it too high. But how simple it would be if we could relax the tension by doffing our ill-fitting corsets and collars! Alas! the trouble is deeper-seated than that.

It is an indisputable and most unfortunate fact that nervous tension registers itself more easily in the muscles about the mouth and throat than anywhere else. So, if we live as do even the children of to-day, under excitement, and so in a state of nervous tension, the habit of speaking with the channel only half open is quickly formed, and the voice becomes shrill and harsh. You have noticed that the more emphatic one grows in argument the higher and harder the voice becomes, and, incidentally, the less convincing the argument. This is true of all excitement; the nervous tension accompanying it constricts the throat, and the result is a closed channel. To learn instinctively to refer this tension for registration not to the throat, but to the diaphragm, is a part of vocal training. This can be easily accomplished with children, and the habit established of taking a deep breath under the influence of any emotion. This breath will cause the throat to open instead of shut, and the tone to grow full, deep, and round, instead of high and harsh. The full, deep, round tone will carry twice as far as the high, harsh, breathy one. The one deep breath resulting in the full, deep tone may—nay, will—often serve the same purpose as Tattycoram's "Count five-and-twenty," and save the angry retort.

It is useless to regret, on either ethical or æsthetic grounds, that we were not taught in childhood to take the deep breath and make the deep tone. But let us look to it that the voices and dispositions of our children are not allowed to suffer. Meanwhile, in correcting the fault in the use of our own instruments, we shall go far toward establishing the proper condition with the next generation, since the child is so mimetic that, to hear sweet, quiet, low tones about him will have more effect than much technical training in keeping his voice free and musical. In the same way, the child who hears good English spoken at home seems less dependent upon text-book in grammar and rhetoric, to perfect his verbal expression, than the child who is not so fortunate in this respect.

To insure the registration of nervous tension in the muscles controlling the diaphragm and not the throat—that is, to form the habit of breathing deeply when speaking under the influence of emotion, is our problem. The present fault in registration will be found to be different with each one of us, or, at least, will cause us "to flock together" according to the place of registration. Each must locate for himself his own difficulty, or go to a vocal specialist and have it located. The tension may be altogether in the muscles governing the throat, or it may be in those about the mouth. There is the resultant, breathy tone, the hard tone, the nasal tone, the guttural tone, the tone that issues from a set jaw or an unruly tongue. All mean tension of muscles somewhere, and must be met by relaxation of these muscles and the freeing of the channel. How to relax the throat shall be our initial point of attack. A suggestion made by my first teacher proved most helpful to me, a suggestion so simple that I did not for the moment take it seriously. "Think," she said, "how your throat feels just before you yawn." "Yes," I replied, irrelevantly, "and just after you have eaten a peppermint — that cool, delicious, open sensation." This impressed her as significant, but not so effective as her suggestion to me, which I felt to be true when I began to think of it seriously, and so, of course, to yawn furiously. Try it.

Think of the yawn. Close your eyes and feel how the deep breath with which the yawn begins (the need of which, indeed, caused it) opens the throat, relaxing all the muscles. Now, instead of yawning, speak. The result

20

will be a good tone, simply because the condition for tone was right. The moment the yawn actually arrives, the condition is lost, the throat closes; but in that moment before the break into the yawn, the muscles about the throat relax and the channel opens, as the muscles controlling the diaphragm tighten and the deep breath is taken.

These, then, are the first exercises in the second step in vocal training. This step is called "Freeing the Tone."

First.—Yawn, noting the sensation.

Second.—Just before the throat breaks into the yawn, stop, and, instead of carrying out the yawn, speak. Repeat this fifty times, three times a day, or twenty times, five times a day, or ten times, as often as you will. Only, keep at it. Take always a single full-vowelled monosyllable: *one*, or *four*, or *no*, or *love*, or *loop*, or *dove*, etc.

We cannot, in this consideration, touch more in detail upon individual cases, but must confine ourselves to these simple exercises, which will, in general, be swiftly and effectively remedial.

But we must not stop with the throat, which is but part of the channel involved in the emission of breath as speech. There is the tense jaw to be reckoned with—the jaw set by nervous tension, the jaw which refuses to yield itself to the moulding of the tone into the beautiful open vowel and the clean-cut consonant which make our words so interesting to utter. It is the set jaw which, forcing the tone to squeeze itself out, causes it to sound thin and hard. Again, it is surrender and not effort I want. Just as I should try to secure the relaxation of your arm or hand by asking you to surrender it to me, drop it a dead weight at your side for me to lift as I choose, so now I ask you to surrender your lower jaw to yourself. Let it go.

Drop your head forward, resting your chin on your chest. Then raise your head, but not your chin. Let your mouth fall open. Assume for the moment that mark of the feeble-minded, the idiotic, the dropped-open mouth, just long enough to note the sensation. Place your fingers on either side of your head where the jaws conjoin, and open your mouth quickly and with intention. Note the action under your finger-tips. Now let the mouth fall open, by simply surrendering the lower jaw, and note this time the lack of action under your fingers, at the juncture of the jaws. It is this passive surrender which we must learn to make, if we find, on investigation, that we are speaking through a half-open mouth held fast by a set jaw. The set jaw resists and distorts the mould, and the beauty of the form of the word which flows from the mould is lost; the relaxed jaw yields to the moulding of the perfectly modelled word.

In practising this relaxation there is very little danger of going too far, since the set jaw is the indication of a tense habit of thought, of a high-strung temperament, and this habit of thought will never become, through the practice of an outward mechanical exercise, the slack habit of thought which is evidenced by the loose dropping of words from a too relaxed jaw—a habit which must be met by quite the opposite method of treatment. There are many exercises involved in vocal training which must be directed very carefully for a time, before the student can be trusted to practise them alone; so I am confining myself in this, as in every step we take together, to the simple, fundamental, and at the same time perfectly safe ones.

To review those for relaxation of the lower jaw:

First.—Drop the head until the chin rests upon the breast. Raise the head, but not the lower jaw:

Second.—With eyes devoid of intelligence and the mouth dropped open, shake the head until you feel the weight of the lower jaw— until the lower jaw seems to hang loosely from the upper jaw and to be shaken by it, as your hand, when you shake it from the wrist, seems to be commanded by the arm, and to have no volition of its own.

Third.—Test your ability to surrender the jaw by placing your fingers on either side your head in front of the ears at the conjunction of the jaws, and first open your mouth with intention, noting the action; then think the word "No," and surrender

24

the jaw to the forming of the word, noting the action or absence of action again.

So much for the set jaw. Ten or fifteen minutes a day—yes, even five minutes a day of actual practice with the constant thought of surrender, will reward you. Try it.

And still the channel is not open. There remains that most unruly member, the tongue—the tongue which refuses to lie flat in the mouth, but insists on rising up when you speak and opposing itself in a little mound at the back of the mouth, over which or around which the tone must creep, or be thrown back into the throat, instead of flowing over the flat or, better still, hollowed surface the tongue should make of itself, to issue an unobstructed column of tone into the mouth, to be moulded by the lips, teeth, and tip of the tongue into beautiful speech-forms. This opposition of the back of the tongue must be fought patiently, persistently, and steadily until the unruly member is conquered. Mirror in hand, stand with a good light on the open mouth. Now concentrate your eyes and thought on the back of the tongue. Then yawn, drinking in the breath, and with the tip of the tongue pressed against your teeth, let your thought suck down the back of the tongue until it forms a little hollow instead of the obstructing mound. If you find response slow to this treatment, if the thought "down" does not result in the concave tongue, touch the obstinate part with the tip of a pencil or any pointed instrument as you think the word "ah." Now try the syllable *la*, *la*, *la*, if necessary, touching the tongue at the back as you speak. Nothing but patient, persistent practice, glass in hand, will carry us successfully past this point in our difficult task of freeing the channel.

To put these directions in exercise form:

First.—Yawn, thinking, the back of the tongue down, as you press the tip against your teeth.

Second.—Touch the back of the tongue with a pencil as you think, or even say, ah.

Third.—Try the syllable *la*, *la*, *la la*, *thinking*, the back of the tongue down, or *touching* it, if necessary.

III

LEARNING TO RE-ENFORCE THE TONE

AND now we turn from the second step in the training to the third and last step—the re-enforcing of the supported and freed tone. It is again a freeing process. This time we are to free the cavities now closed against the tone; we are to use the walls of these cavities as sounding-boards for tone, as they were designed to be, so re-enforcing the tone and letting it issue a resonant, bell-like note with the carrying power resonance alone can give, instead of the thin, dull, colorless sound which conveys no life to the word into which it is moulded by the organs of speech. How shall we free these cavities? I find myself now impatient of the medium of communication we are using. I want to make the tone for you. I want, for

27

instance, to shut off the nasal cavity and let you hear the resultant nasal note, thin, high, unresonant, which hardly reaches the first member of my audience; then I want you to hear the tone flood into the nasal cavity, and, re-enforced there by the vibration from the walls of the cavity, grow a resonant, ringing, bell-like note, which will carry to the farthest corner of the room without the least increase in loudness. But we must be content with the conditions imposed by print.

First, you must realize that so-called "talking through the nose" is not talking *through* the nose at all, but rather failure to do so— that is, instead of letting the tone flood into the nasal cavity, to be re-enforced there by striking against the walls of the cavity, which act as sounding-boards for the tone confined within that cavity, we shut off the cavity, and refuse the tone its natural re-enforcement. It takes on, as a result, a thin, unresonant quality which we call nasal, although it is thin and unpleasing because it *lacks true nasal resonance*. The only remedy lies in ceasing to shut off the cavity. Think the sound ŏŏ. Let the tone on which it is to be borne grow slowly in thought, filling, filling, and, as it grows, flooding the whole face. Let it press against your lips (in thought only as yet), feel your nostrils expand, your face grow alive between the eyes and the upper lip, that area so often inanimate, lifeless, even in a mobile, animated countenance. Now let the sound come, but let it follow the thought, flood the face, let the nostrils expand, feel the nasal cavity fill with sound; let it go on up into the head and strike the forehead and the eye-sockets and the walls of all the cavities so unused to the impact of sound, which should never have been shut out. Now begin, with lips closed, a humming note, *m-m-m*. Let it come flooding into the face, until it presses against the lips, demanding the open mouth. Now let it open the mouth into the ah. Repeat this over and over — *m*-ah, *m-ah*, *m-ah*. Don't let the tone drop back as the mouth opens. Keep it forward behind the upper lip, which it has made full, and which, playing against, it tickles until we *must* let the tone escape. Just as much of the day as possible, think the tone in a flood into the face, and as often as possible hum and let it escape, noting its increasing resonance. It will increase in resonance, I promise you. It will lose its thin, high-pitched nasal quality, and grow mellow and rich and ringing.

And so, with chest lifted, diaphragm at work, throat open, tongue flat, jaws relaxed, and all the cavities concerned in vocalization open to the tone, as you breathe and yawn and hum, let it issue a full, round, resonant, singing note to add itself to the music of the world.

PART II

THE TECHNIQUE OF THE INSTRUMENT

I

DISCUSSION

WE leave, then, the question of the tuning of the instrument to turn to a consideration of its technique when tuned. I invite you to enter with me upon a study of the vocal interpretation of literature, through which, as I have said, the voice, put to its highest use, may be made the beautiful agent of personality it is intended to be. This term, "vocal interpretation of literature," has been criticised as a sesquipedalian way of designating the good, old-fashioned exercise, "reading aloud." I wish the criticism were pertinent. It is not, because however identical in theory these exercises may be, in practice they are horribly opposed. So far apart are they, indeed, that we are told to beware of the reader who calls himself an "Interpreter." On the contrary, we should beware of the reader who has not established his claim to be an interpreter. The only excuse in the world for the existence of a reader lies in the possession of superior powers of interpretation. Unless I can make clear what must otherwise for some remain obscure, make beautiful what otherwise for some must remain commonplace, make alive what otherwise for some must lie dead on the printed page, I, as a reader, have no reason for being. To do any or all of these things is precisely to be an interpreter. However, we are entering upon this study of interpretation, not with the idea of becoming public readers, but with the intention of perfecting our voices.

There is a theory that it is dangerous to go beyond the mere freeing of the instrument in either vocal or physical training. In accordance with this theory I was advised by a well-known actress to confine my study for the stage, so far as the vocal and pantomimic preparation was concerned, to singing, dancing, and fencing. "Get your voice and body under control," she said, "make them

free, but don't connect shades of thought and
emotion with definite tones of the voice or
movements of the body; don't meddle with
Delsarte or elocution." This advice seemed
good at the time. It still seems to me that
it ought to be the right method. But I have
grown to distrust it. One of the chief sources
of my distrust has been the effect of the
theory upon the art of the actress who gave
the advice. She is perhaps the most graceful woman on the stage to-day, and her voice
is pure music. But her gestures and tones
fail in lucidity; they fail to illumine the text
of the part she essays to interpret. One
grows suddenly impatient of the meaningless
grace of her movements, the meaningless
music of her voice. One longs for a swift—
if studied—stride across the stage in anger,
instead of the unstudied grace of her glide
in swirling-robed protest. One longs to hear
a staccato declaration of intention, instead
of the cadenced music of a voice guiltless
of intention. No! after the body has been
made a free and responsive agent, a mastery of certain fundamental laws, a mastery

of certain principles of gesture in accordance with the dictates of thought and emotion is necessary to its further perfecting as a vivid, powerful, and true agent of personality. The action must be suited to the word, the word to the action, through a study of the laws governing expression in action.

So with the voice: to become not only a free instrument, but a beautiful and powerful means of expression and commnuication, it must learn to recognize and obey certain fundamental laws governing its modulations. A master of verbal expression is distinguished by his vast vocabulary of words, and his skill and discrimination in its use. A master of vocal expression must acquire what we may call a vocal vocabulary, consisting of changes of pitch, varieties of inflection, and variations in tone-color, and must know how to use these elements with skill and discrimination. It is through a study of the vocal interpretation of literature that such a vocabulary is to be acquired. To learn to command at will the changes of pitch and variations of inflection and tone-color which subtle

36

shades of thought and feeling demand, is the final step to be mastered in training the voice.

I have long held that a substitution of vocal interpretation of literature for a large proportion of the subjects now taught in our public schools would solve an equal proportion of the problems confronting our educators. I believe this study, properly conducted, involves the finest kind of mental, emotional, physical, and ethical discipline. I believe that a child put into training at six, in a school which made this subject the beginning and end and main body of its curriculum, would find himself at sixteen, with mind disciplined, imagination untrammelled, emotions free, controlled, and unafraid, voice and body responsive agents, and with "knowledge absolute, subject to no dispute," of his own bent and an eager enthusiasm in pursuing it. Do not dismiss this as the extravagance of an enthusiast. At least, reserve judgment until you have traced with me the process of transferring through the voice (vocally interpreting) real thought (literature) from the printed page to the mind of an auditor. The main object of the exercise will be, of course, to mark its effect upon the voice. But in order to establish the broader claim I am making for the study, I ask you to consider, as well, the mental, emotional, and ethical training involved. It would, indeed, be difficult to study one without the other, since it is the play of an elastic mind, controlled emotion, and a quickened spirit upon the voice which is to make the free and responsive instrument an effective agent. It is through the process of which we are about to make a study that the mind is made elastic, the emotions set free, and the spirit quickened. It is the act of intense concentration and strong transition demanded of the mind by this process which will deepen and broaden its action; it is the swift response and perfect control demanded of the emotions by this process which will steady and free their play; it is the constant dwelling in an atmosphere of truth and beauty demanded of the spirit by this process which will quicken its life. These effects upon mind, heart, soul, and voice are simultaneous, and cannot be separated out in our study of the act which produces them. Then, in entering upon this step in vocal training, let us mentally drive a four-in-hand.

We must begin by choosing a passage for interpretation. What shall govern our choice? It must be a passage worth interpreting, or we shall not be dealing with literature, and so shall not meet the requirements of our title. To be worth interpreting, it must possess one or combine all of these three attributes—beauty, truth, and power. And here at once, as a point in our minor claim, note the ethical training demanded of the student by this subject. Surely to dwell appreciatively many hours of each day in an atmosphere charged with beauty, truth, and power is to be quickened spiritually or to be a dull clod indeed.

How will this passage from Emerson's essay on Friendship do for our experiment:

"Our friendships hurry to short and poor conclusions, because we have made them a texture of wine and dreams, instead of the tough fibre of the human heart."

It is certainly truth beautifully and powerfully expressed. Surely it will serve. And here I should like to stop and discuss with you that vital question of choosing literature for children, according to temperament and age—but another time, perhaps.

Having read the passage under consideration cursorily (as is the custom in reading to one's self to-day), will you now study it for a moment very closely? Now, once more, please, read it silently, noting the action of your mind as you read. ("Watch its pulsations," Dr. Curry would say.) And now aloud, although without an auditor, read it, this time noting the effect of the action of the mind upon your voice. Did its pitch change? Where and why? How did you inflect the words "wine and dreams"? How did the inflection of these words differ from that of the last six words, "tough fibre of the human heart," with which they are contrasted in thought? Did your tone change color at any point? Why? Where? But now, once more, let us approach the passage, this time with a different intention. Let us

study it with the idea of interpreting it for another mind. Now the method of attack is very different. Not that it ought to be different! But it is. Intense concentration ought to characterize all our reading, whether its object be to acquire knowledge or pleasure for one's self, or to impart either to another. But the day of reading which "maketh a full man" seems to be long past, so far as the general public is concerned. The necessity of skimming the pages of a dozen fourth-rate books of the hour, in order to be at least a lucid interlocutor and so a desired dinner guest, is making our reading a swift gathering of colorless impressions which may remain a week or only a day, and which leave no lasting effect of beauty or truth upon the mind and heart of the reader. Should it not be rather an intense application of the mind to the thought of a master-mind, until that thought, in all its power and beauty, has broadened the boundaries of the reader's mind and enlarged the meaning of all his thoughts? I wonder if a much smaller proportion of time spent in such reading might not result in a less "bromidic" social atmosphere even though its tendency were a bit serious. Who knows?

But let us return to Emerson on Friendship. In studying this thought for the purpose of interpreting it vocally, the concentration of the attention must be intense, because I must make it absolutely my own before I can present it to you. It must, for the moment, possess me. It must seem, for the time, to be a creation of my own brain. It must belong to me as only the created thing can. Until I have so recreated the thought, it is not mine to give. Now read the passage silently with this idea of making it your own. Pour upon it the light of your experience, your philosophy, your ideals, your perception of truth. Comment upon it silently as you read. Now read it aloud and let your voice do this commenting. But wait a moment. Let me quote for you the paragraph following this statement:

"The laws of friendship are austere and eternal, of one web with the laws of nature and of morals. But we have aimed at a swift and petty benefit, to suck a sudden sweetness. We snatch at the slowest fruit in the whole garden of God, which many summers and many winters must ripen."

This is Emerson's paraphrase of his original statement. How much of it did your mental commentary include? How did your silent paraphrase resemble this? Read the original passage again to yourself in the light of this paraphrase. I shall ask you now to repeat the first sentence from memory, for you will find, after this concentrated contemplation of a thought, that its form is fixed fast in your mind. That is a delightful accompaniment of this kind of reading. The form of the thought, if it be apposite (which it must be to be literature, and we are considering only literature), the form of a thought so approached stays with us in all its beauty.

Let us then repeat the original statement, having read the passage in which Emerson has elaborated it. Now, what you must demand of your voice is this: that it shall so handle the single introductory sentence as to suggest the rest of the paragraph. In other words, your voice must do the paraphrasing,

43

by means of its changes in pitch, its inflections, and its variations in tone-color. Once
more read the sentence casually as you did
at first, as a mere statement of fact, and then
again in this paraphrastical manner. Watch,
watch, watch the voice. Mark the growth
of its light and shade with the second reading.

We must not lose sight of our minor claim.
But the mental and ethical training involved
has been too obvious, I am sure, to have
escaped us. We need go back for but a moment to renote it. The intense concentration and strong transition of thought required
of the mind, in mastering a text for the purpose of interpretation, afford keen intellectual
exercise. The underlying idea in approaching a passage full of truth and beauty,
that the knowledge or pleasure I gain from
it is not for the purpose of self-gratification,
but that I may share it with another, is of
great ethical value. Especially is this true
in teaching children the laws of vocal expression.

II

STUDY IN CHANGE OF PITCH

LET us now confine our work to a study in
change of pitch, which is the fundamental
element of the vocal vocabulary we are en-
deavoring to acquire. Had I an actual class
before me, I should now divide your voices
into groups according to the varying degrees
of grayness. As it is, I must treat you all
as monotones. For our present purpose we
should choose a passage which, to be intelligently interpreted, demands marked changes
of pitch. Robert Browning affords the best
material of this kind, because of his sudden
and long-sustained parentheses, which can be
handled lucidly by the voice only after it has
mastered this fundamental element of a vocal vocabulary. Let us take the first stanza

and the first line of the second stanza of "Abt Vogler":

"Would that the structure brave, the manifold music I build,
Bidding my organ obey, calling its keys to their work,
Claiming each slave of the sound, at a touch, as when Solomon willed
Armies of angels that soar, legions of demons that lurk,
Man, brute, reptile, fly—alien of end and of aim,
Adverse, each from the other heaven - high, hell-deep removed,
Should rush into sight at once as he named the ineffable Name,
And pile him a palace straight, to pleasure the princess he loved!

"Would it might tarry like his, the beautiful building of mine—"

Remember, we are to confine our consideration to the one point, "change of pitch," not the change of pitch *within a word*, which is *inflection* and belongs to another chapter, but to the *broad* changes of pitch from word to word, phrase to phrase, sentence to sentence, following the intricate changes of the thought. With this end in mind, let us first blaze a trail through this forest of ideas. Let us find the main road and then trace the by-paths which lead away from that main road, and in this case fortunately come back to it again—which does not always happen in Mr. Browning's "woody tracts of thought." To employ a better figure for vocal purposes, let us cut off the stream, the voice, and trace the bed of this river of thought, following the main channel, and then its branches. We find the main channel cut by the first and last lines:

"Would that the structure brave, the manifold music I build,

.   .   .   .   .   .

Would it might tarry like his, the beautiful building of mine—"

All between, beginning with the second line, "Bidding my organ obey," and including the last words of the eighth line, "the princess he loved," is a branch channel, leading away from and coming back to the main river's bed. But this branch channel is interrupted in turn by its own branch leading away from

it and returning with it to join the main bed
with the last line we quote. ·This second
branch begins in the middle of the third line
with the words, "as when Solomon willed,"
wanders in this course for five lines, and,
rejoining the first offshoot, returns to the
main channel with the last line. Now let us
turn on the stream, the voice, and watch it
flow into the course as traced. What happens? Dropping the figure, the voice starts
on a certain pitch, determined by the atmosphere of the main thought, modified by the
parentheses. If the main thought were not
interrupted, the original pitch might be much
lower. But we must make allowance for the
necessity of dropping the voice for each of
the two parentheses. We must, therefore,
start on a comparatively high pitch, from
which we may depart easily at the end of
the first line, where the secondary thought
begins, and to which we return, after a second drop, with the last line, which resumes
the main thought. Let us try this. Carry the
exact pitch, with which you start, over the
parentheses, and begin the last line on the

48

original pitch. Can you do it? If you can
you are not a monotone. But you may need
the exercise just the same, for there are many
degrees of dulness in tone. Now let us take
up the parentheses. The first one begins
with the second line. The voice must drop
on the words, "Bidding my organ obey," to
a lower pitch, indicating instantly the interruption of the thought. Hold this pitch
through the second line and until the last
four words of the third line. With these
words, "as when Solomon willed," the voice
falls upon the second interruption, which it
must denote by a corresponding second drop
in pitch. This it pursues until it reaches the
last line, where it resumes the original pitch
with the original thought. Try this. These
are only the broad changes from sentence to
sentence. There are lesser changes from
phrase to phrase, partly for the sake of variety alone, as in the second and third lines,
where the pitch changes after "obey," runs
through the next six words, "calling its keys
to their work," and returns again on, "Claiming each slave of the sound." There is also

49

a momentary lift of the voice on the three words "at a touch," dropping to the second broad change with the next words, "as when Solomon willed." Try this more detailed treatment of the first parenthesis. Taking up the second interruption for this closer study: The parenthesis begins with the last three words of the third line, as we have said. The voice starting with this second drop in pitch, plays about the level of that pitch from phrase to phrase through five lines, but it also changes from word to word, as on the four closing the fifth line, "Man, brute, reptile, fly," and this time merely for the sake of variety. Remember, whatever the departure, it must always follow the parenthetical thought, bringing it back by resuming the original pitch, from which it departed to indicate the interruption.

Will you not diagram these nine lines? Simply write the verse as prose, and then mark it for change of pitch. Call the original pitch C, the first broad change B, the second broad change A. Denote the changes within the parentheses by sharps and flats.

STUDY IN CHANGE OF PITCH

For instance, would not the pitch of the last three words of the second line be indicated correctly by marking it B-sharp? But do not stop with the diagram. Begin and end by testing the voice. Make it follow the changes you indicate on the diagram, until it masters the subtlest of them. Through such practice alone can you hope to increase the light and shade upon which the voice depends for its final beauty as an agent of personality.

III

TO me, the most notable among the many notable elements in Madame Alla Nazimova's marvellous acting is her illumination of the text of her impersonations through *inflection*. To an ear unaccustomed to the "broken music" of her speech, a word may now and then be lost because of her still faulty English, but of her attitude toward the thought she is uttering, or the person she is addressing, or the situation she is meeting, there can never be a moment's doubt—so illuminating is the inflectional play of her voice. The tone she uses is not to me pleasing in quality. It does not fall in liquid alluring cadences upon the ear as does Miss Marlowe's, for instance. It is always keyed high, whether the child-wife Nora, or Hedda omnivorous of experience, is speaking. But this high-pitched tone is endlessly volatile. It is restless. It never lets your attention wander. It is never monotonous. It is a master of inflection. Madame Nazimova's emotion is always primarily intellectual. It always proceeds from a mind keenly alive to the instant's incident. This intensely intellectual temperament reveals itself through her voice in a rare degree of inflectional agility. This element alone makes her work, to me, more stimulating than any I have ever known except Madame Duse's. Recall the revelation of Nora's soul in her cry: "It is not possible! It is not possible!" Madame Nazimova's conception of the mistress of "The Doll's House" is concentrated in these four words—in her inflection of the last word, I may almost say. When I close my eyes and think of Madame Nazimova's voice, I see a grove of soft maples in early October with the sun playing upon them; while Miss Marlowe's tone carries me at once into the pine woods, where a white birch now and then shimmers its yellow leaves. Again,

53

the voice of the Russian actress suggests a handful of diamonds, and the American instrument a set of turquoise in the matrix. The difference in these two agents of two compelling personalities is, of course, the result of a difference in the two temperaments; but undoubtedly it also arises from a difference. in methods of training. Whatever the temperament, light and shade can be developed in the voice through practice of inflection; and whatever the temperament, a pure tone can be secured through a mastery of support of breath and freedom of vocal conditions. The voices of these two actresses vividly illustrate these two points. We have studied how to secure Miss Marlowe's tone. We are now to work for Madame Nazimova's light and shade, so far as a mastery of inflection will secure it. How shall we proceed?

"All my life," writes Ellen Terry, in her entrancing memoirs, "the thing which has struck me as wanting on the stage is variety. Some people are tone deaf, and they find it physically impossible to observe the law of contrasts. But even a physical deficiency can be overcome by that faculty of taking infinite pains." That is the secret of successful acquisition in any direction, is it not —the "faculty of taking infinite pains"? With Ellen Terry it resulted in a voice which in its prime estate suggested, it is said, all the riotous colors of all the autumns, or Henry Ward Beecher's most varied collection of precious stones. We can secure an approximate result by employing the same method. Let us proceed with "infinite pains" to practise, practise, practise *inflection*.

Let us first examine this "change of pitch within a word" which we call inflection. How does the pitch change, and why, and what does the change indicate? We have discovered that a change of thought results in a broad change of pitch from word to word, phrase to phrase, sentence to sentence, and we shall discover that a change in emotion results in a change in the color of the tone we are using; but this element of our vocal vocabulary, *inflection*, is subtler than

55

either of the other two. While change of pitch is an intellectual modulation, and variation in tone-color is an emotional modulation, inflection, in a degree, combines both. It is a change in both color and key within the word. It is primarily of intellectual significance, but it also reveals certain temperamental characteristics which cannot be disassociated with emotion. For instance, the staccato utterance of Mrs. Fiske is technically the result of her use of straight, swift-falling inflections, but it is temperamentally the result of thinking and feeling in terms of Becky Sharp.

Let us see how inflections vary. They rise and fall swiftly or slowly. They move in a straight line from point to point, or make a curve. (The latter we call circumflex inflection.) They make various angles with the original level of pitch, rising or falling abruptly or gradually. These are some of the variations, each indicating an attitude of the mind and heart of the speaker toward the thought, or toward the one spoken to, or toward the circumstances out of which the speech arises. All must be mastered for use at will if light and shade are to be developed in the voice.

Now let us take a phrase or sentence, and voice it under a certain condition, noting the inflection of the word or words which hold the thought of the phrase or sentence in solution. Then let us change the condition and again voice the thought, noting the change in inflection. Let me propound again the profound question asked in our first lesson: Do you like growing old? The answers will all be "yes" or "no." But what of the inflection of those monosyllabic words? Sweet Sixteen will employ a straight, swift-falling inflection on the affirmative (unless some untoward influence, such as "Love the Destroyer," has embittered her life, when she may give us one of May Iverson's adorable replies, masked in indifference and circumlocution). Twenty will employ the straight-falling inflection without the swiftness of Sweet Sixteen's slide. With twenty-five we detect a faint sign of a curve in the more gradual fall. Twenty-eight to thirty-five em-

57

ploys various degrees of circumflex, according to the desire — or possibility — of concealing the real facts. Forty to forty-five, if in defiant mood, employs the abrupt-falling inflection, or, if quite honest, changes to the negative with as swift and straight a fall. This lasts through sixty-five, and at seventy we hear a new and gentle circumflex on the "no," until the pride of extreme old age sets in at eighty-five with the swift fall of Sixteen's affirmative. Were it not expedient to maintain friendly relations with one's printer, I should venture to diagram these changes of tone within a word. As it is, I shall content myself with advising you to do so.

It is my privilege to have had acquaintance with a woman who was a personal friend of Emerson. Among the incidents of his delightful talk to her, retold to me, I recall one which bears upon our present problem. They were discussing mutual "Friends on the Shelf." "Have you ever read *Titan?*" asked the gentle seer. "Yes," replied the lady. "Read it again!" said he. Query to the class: How did the lady inflect the word "Yes" to call forth the injunction, "Read it again"? What did her inflection reveal?

However inclined we may be to quarrel with Bernhardt's conception of the Duke of Reichstadt, we can never forget her disclosure of the Eaglet's frail soul *through inflection* as she crushes letter after letter in her hand and tosses them aside, uttering the single word, "Destroyed," and the final revelation in the quick, thrilling curve of her wonderful voice on the same word as the little cousin leaves the room at the close of this episode of the letters.

No better material can be chosen for a study of inflection than the paragraph from Emerson's "Friendship," quoted in a preceding chapter. Let us repeat the first sentence again. "Our friendships hurry to short and poor conclusions because we have made them a texture of wine and dreams instead of the tough fibre of the human heart." Study, in voicing this, how to illumine the thought by your contrastive inflection of the words "wine and dreams" and "tough fibre of the human heart." A lingering circumflex cadence in uttering the first two words will suggest the unstable nature of a friendship woven out of so frail a fabric as wine and dreams, while a swift, strong, straight-falling inflection on each of the last six words indicates the vigorous growth of a love rooted in the tough fibre of the human heart.

In "Monna Vanna," Maurice Maeterlinck gives the actress a superb opportunity to show her mastery of inflection. Let us turn to the scene in Prinzivalle's tent:[1]

"PRINZIVALLE. Are you in pain?

"VANNA. No!

"PRINZIVALLE. Will you let me have it [her wound] dressed?

"VANNA. No! (*Pause.*)

"PRINZIVALLE. You are decided?

"VANNA. Yes.

"PRINZIVALLE. Need I recall the terms of the—?

"VANNA. It is useless—I know them.

"PRINZIVALLE. Your lord consents.

"VANNA. Yes.

"PRINZIVALLE. It is my mind to leave you free. . . .

"There is yet time should you desire to renounce. . . .

"VANNA. No!"

[1] From "Monna Vanna." By Maurice Maeterlinck. Published by Harper & Brothers.

STUDY IN INFLECTION

And so the seeming inquisition proceeds. To each relentlessly searching interrogation from Gianello comes Vanna's unfaltering reply, in a single, swift monosyllable, "Yes" or "No." The same word, but, oh, the revelation which may lie in the inflection of that word! Let us try it. Let us read the scene aloud, first giving as nearly as possible the same inflection to each of Vanna's answers, then let us voice it again, putting into the curve of the tone within the narrow space of the two or three lettered monosyllables all the concentrated mental passion of Vanna's soul in its attitude toward the terrible situation and toward the man whom she believes to be her enemy. This is a most difficult exercise, but if "a man's reach should exceed his grasp," it will not retard our progress toward the goal of a vocal vocabulary to attempt it now. Apart from all aim in its pursuit, there is no more fascinating study than this study of inflection. In this day of artistic photography there is an endless interest for the artist of the camera in playing with a subject's expression by varying the

light and shade thrown upon the face. So
for the student of vocal expression there is
endless interest in this play, with the thought
behind a group of words, by varying the inflection of those words. Lady Macbeth's,
"We fail!" or Macbeth's, "If it were done
when 'tis done, then 'twere well it were done
quickly," occurs to us, of course, as rich
material for this exercise.

In her analysis of the character of Lady
Macbeth, Mrs. Jameson gives us an interesting "Study in Inflection," based on Mrs.
Siddons's interpretation of the words "We
fail." A foot-note reads: "In her impersonation of the part of Lady Macbeth, Mrs.
Siddons adopted successively three different
intonations in giving the words 'we fail.'
At first a quick, contemptuous interrogation
—'we fail?' Afterward with the note of
admiration—'we fail!' and an accent of
indignant astonishment laying the principal
emphasis on the word we—'*we* fail!' Lastly,
she fixed on what I am convinced is the true
reading—'*we fail.*'—with the simple period,
modulating the voice to a deep, low, resolute

tone which settled the issue at once, as though she had said: 'If we fail, why then we fail, and all is over.'"

Think how vitally the total impersonation is affected by your choice of inflections at this point. Compare the effects of the three Mrs. Siddons tested. Are there other possible intonations of the words? What are they? Do you realize the vital effect upon the voice of such vocal analysis and experimentation? Devote ten minutes of the time you take for reading each day to this phase of vocal interpretation, and at the end of a week note its effect upon your silent reading and upon your voice.

Remember, with inflection, as with every other phase of the training, the greatest immediate benefit will come from holding the question of its peculiar significance constantly in mind. Study the temperament of the people about you by noting this element in their speech. Study the attitude of every interlocutor you face, by studying the inflection of his replies to the questions of life and death you propound. But, above all, study your own use of this element. Do not let your own attitude go undetected. It may help you to alter an unfortunate attitude to realize its effect upon your own voice.

IV

STUDY IN TONE-COLOR

AND now we must turn to our last point of discussion, Tone-color. What is the nature of this element of our vocabulary— this *Klangfarbe*, this *Timbre?* Upon what does it depend? You will say, "It is a property of the voice depending upon the form of the vibrations which produce the tone." True! And physiologically the form of the vibrations depends upon the condition of the entire vocal apparatus. Tone-color, then, is a modulation of resonance. But what concerns us is the fact that it is an emotional modulation of resonance. What concerns us is the fact that, as a change of thought instantly registers itself in a change of pitch, so a change of emotion instantly produces a change in the color of the tone—if the voice

65

is a free instrument. And so, as before, I want you not to think of the physiological aspect, but to yield to the emotion, noting the character of the resultant tone, regardless of what has happened in the larynx to produce that result.

As Browning affords us the best material for our study in change of pitch, so the poems of Sidney Lanier offer to the voice the richest field for exercise in tone-color. Musician and poet in one, Lanier's peculiar charm lies in his unerring choice of words, which suggest in their sound, when rightly voiced, the atmosphere of the scene he is painting. Lanier uses words as Corot uses colors. This gives the voice its opportunity to bring out by subtle variations in *timbre* the variations in light and shade of an atmosphere. To read aloud, sympathetically, once a day, Lanier's "The Symphony" is the best possible way to develop simultaneously all the elements of a vocal vocabulary. We shall use this poem to-day as a text for our study in tone-color. Let us omit the message of the violins and heavier strings, and take the passage beginning with the interlude upon which the flute-voice breaks:

"But presently
A velvet flute-note fell down pleasantly
Upon the bosom of that harmony,
And sailed and sailed incessantly,
As if a petal from a wild rose blown
Had fluttered down upon that pool of tone
And boatwise dropped o' the convex side
And floated down the glassy tide
And clarified and glorified
The solemn spaces where the shadows bide.
From the warm concave of that fluted note
Somewhat, half song, half odor, forth did float,
As if a rose might somehow be a throat."

What an ideal for tone-color! Dare we think to make it ours? We must. We must adopt it with confidence of attainment. Let me quote a little further:

"When Nature from her far-off glen
Flutes her soft messages to men,
The flute can say them o'er again;
Yea, Nature, singing sweet and lone,
Breathes through life's strident polyphone
The flute-voice in the world of tone."

Read this passage aloud as a mere statement of fact, employing a matter-of-fact tone. Gray in color, is it not? Now let your voice take the color Lanier has blended for you Let your tone, like a thing "half song, half odor," float forth on these words and linger as only a perfume can about the thought. Now let the tone change in color to clarify and glorify the following message from the flute:[1]

"Sweet friends,
Man's love ascends
To finer and diviner ends
Than man's mere thought e'er comprehends."

I cannot, for lack of space, reprint the whole flute message, but you will get the poem, if you have it not, and voice every word of it, I am sure. Here are some of the most telling lines for our present purpose:

"I speak for each no-tongued tree
That, spring by spring, doth nobler be,
And dumbly and most wistfully
His mighty prayerful arms outspreads
Above men's oft-unheeding heads,
And his big blessing downward sheds.
I speak for all-shaped blooms and leaves,
Lichens on stones and moss on eaves,
Grasses and grains in ranks and sheaves;

[1] The extracts on pp. 67–74 are from Mr. Sidney Lanier's volume of "Poems," published by Charles Scribner's Sons.

Broad-fronded ferns and keen-leaved canes,
And briery mazes bounding lanes,
And marsh-plants, thirsty-cupped for rains,
And milky stems and sugary veins;
For every long-armed woman-vine
That round a piteous tree doth twine;
For passionate odors, and divine
Pistils, and petals crystalline;
.   .   .   .   .   .
All tree-sounds, rustlings of pine-cones,
Wind-sighings, doves' melodious moans,
And night's unearthly undertones;
All placid lakes and waveless deeps,
All cool, reposing mountain-steeps,
Vale-calms and tranquil lotos-sleeps;—
Yea, all fair forms, and sounds, and lights,
And warmths, and mysteries, and mights,
Of Nature's utmost depths and heights,
—These doth my timid tongue present,
Their mouthpiece and leal instrument
And servant, all love-eloquent."

You see, to voice this message, a mood born of all the "warmths and mysteries and mights of Nature's utmost depths and heights" must take possession of you, and you must yield your instrument to the expression of that mood. Then watch, watch, watch the color of the tone change as the voice, starting with the clear flute-note, follows sympathetically the varying phases of Nature's face which the poet has so sympathetically painted. And now, after a "thrilling calm," the flute yields its place to a sister instrument, and the tone must change its *timbre* to the reed note of the clarionet. In the "melting" message of that instrument we find two passages which afford the voice chance for a most vivid contrast in color. Beginning with the line, "Now comes a suitor with sharp, prying eye," read the two descriptions which follow, lending your voice to the atmosphere of each:

"Says, Here, you Lady, if you'll sell I'll buy:
  Come, heart for heart—a trade? What! weeping?
    why?
  Shame on such wooer's dapper mercery!
  I would my lover kneeling at my feet
  In humble manliness should cry, O sweet!
  I know not if thy heart my heart will greet:
  I ask not if thy love my love can meet:
  Whate'er thy worshipful soft tongue shall say,
  I'll kiss thine answer, be it yea or nay:
  I do but know I love thee, and I pray
  To be thy knight until my dying day."

The first two lines, which set forth a suit in terms of trade, demand a hard, calculating

tone, suggestive of large silver dollars. Call
this color dull steel gray. This tone flashes
out for a moment in the white indignation
of the third line, softens and warms with the
next two lines, then grows and glows until
it reaches a crimson radiance in the last two
lines. Try it!

And now, with "heartsome voice of mellow scorn," let us sound the message of the
"bold straightforward horn."

" ' Now comfort thee,' said he,
    ' Fair Lady.
For God shall right thy grievous wrong,
And man shall sing thee a true-love song,
Voiced in act his whole life long,
Yea, all thy sweet life long,
    Fair Lady.

" ' Where's he that craftily hath said
The day of chivalry is dead?
I'll prove that lie upon his head,
Or I will die instead,
    Fair Lady.

Now by each knight that e'er hath prayed
To fight like a man and love like a maid,
Since Pembroke's life as Pembroke's blade,
I' the scabbard, death was laid,

THE SPEAKING VOICE

I dare avouch my faith is bright
That God doth right and God hath might.
Nor time hath changed His hair to white,
Nor His dear love to spite,
    Fair Lady.

" ' I doubt no doubts: I strive and shrive my clay,
  And fight my fight in the patient, modern way
  For true love and for thee—ah me! and pray
  To be thy knight until my dying day,
    Fair Lady.'

" Made end that knightly horn, and spurred away,
  Into the thick of the melodious fray."

Remember your "key" is set for you; the color of the tone is plainly chosen for you by Mr. Lanier. Not red nor yellow, but a blending of the two. *Orange*, is it not? Will not an orange tone give us the feel of heartsome confidence behind and through the mellow scorn of the knight's message? Try it! Let the two primary colors, red and yellow, enter in varying degrees according to, or following, the emotional variation in the thought, as the knight or the lover dominates in the message. In the first seven lines, the tone glows with the love radiance and the orange deepens toward red. With the next five lines the lover yields to the knight, and the tone flashes forth a golden, keen-edged sword. With the thirteenth line the tone begins in the orange on, "Now by each knight that e'er hath prayed," flashes into yellow in "to fight like a man," softens and deepens toward red in "and love like a maid," and returns to the orange to finish the horn motive.

Next in this poem which affords such a wonderful study for tone-color, we have the hautboy's message. The color is mixed and laid on the palette ready for use as before, with the introductory lines:

> "And then the hautboy played and smiled,
> And sang like any large-eyed Child,
> Cool-hearted and all undefiled."

Don't let the words "large-eyed Child" mislead you. Don't, I beseech you, make the mistake of adopting the "Little Orphan Annie" tone with which the "elocutionist" too often insults the pure treble of a child's "undefiled" instrument. That is the keynote to us for our choice of color—"cool-hearted and all undefiled." Almost a white tone, is it not? With a little of the blue of the June sky? Try it. Let the blue be visibly present in the first three lines:

> "'Huge Trade!' he said,
> 'Would thou wouldst lift me on thy head
> And run where'er my finger led!'"

turning to pure white in the next three lines:

> "Once said a Man—and wise was He—
> Never shalt thou the heavens see
> Save as a little child thou be."

The last voice comes from the "ancient wise bassoons." Again there is danger. Do not, oh! do not fall afoul of the conventional old man's quavering tone. There is nothing conventional about these "weird, gray-beard old harpers sitting on the high sea-dunes," chanting runes. The last words of these introductory lines safeguard us — "chanted runes." There is only one color of tone in which to "chant runes." Gray, is it not? Yes, but a silver gray, not the steel gray of the clarionet when she became for the moment a commercial lover. Then in the silver-gray tone of the philosopher, voice this last motive:

> " Bright-waved gain, gray-waved loss,
> The sea of all doth lash and toss,
> One wave forward and one across:
> But now 'twas trough, now 'tis crest,
> And worst doth foam and flash to best,
>   And curst to blest.

The importance of a right use of tone-color in vocal interpretation was impressed upon a Browning class last winter. We were reading the *Dramatic Lyrics*. The poem for the hour was "Meeting at Night." The tone with which the first student attacked this exquisite love-lyric was so businesslike, so matter of fact, so utterly out of key, that we who listened saw not the lover hastening to his beloved, but a real-estate agent "out to buy" a farm. The "gray sea, the long black land, the yellow half-moon large and low, the startled little waves that creep in fiery ringlets from their sleep, the pushing prow of the boat quenched in the slushy sand, the warm, sea-scented beach, and the three fields" all assumed a merely commercial value. They were interesting exactly as would be a catalogue of properties in a deed of real estate. If you are not a very "intense" member of a Browning society you will, I think, enjoy the test of tone-color involved in reading this poem from the contrasted standpoints of the business man and the lover. Of course, in the first instance you must stop where I, in desperation, stopped the student on the words, "a farm appears." For I defy any one to read the last two lines in a gray, matter-of-fact tone.

As was the case in our consideration of inflection, so in this study of tone-color there is an embarrassment of rich material for the exercise of this element. Lanier's "Sunrise" and "Corn"; Browning's "Prologue" to "The Two Poets of Croisic," with a vivid contrast of color in each verse; Swinburne's almost every line; Dante Gabriel Rossetti, Wordsworth, Keats, Tennyson — but why enumerate? All the colorists among the poets will reward your search of a text for the development of *timbre*.

STUDY IN TONE-COLOR

For a final brief study of the three elements we aim to acquire, with especial emphasis in thought upon the last one, let us take this prologue to "The Two Poets of Croisic," with its color-contrast in each verse:

> "Such a starved bank of moss
>   Till that May morn,
>   Blue ran the flash across:
>   Violets were born!
>
> "Sky—what a scowl of cloud
>   Till, near and far,
>   Ray on ray split the shroud:
>   Splendid, a star!
>
> "World—how it walled about
>   Life with disgrace
>   Till God's own smile came out:
>   That was thy face!"

The vocal treatment of the first two verses will be very much alike. The voice starts in minor key, a gray monotone, in harmony with the absence of color in the bare bank of dull moss. The inflection of the word "starved" must emphasize the grayness. It must be a dull push of the tone on the first syllable, with little, if any, lift above the level of the low pitch on which the whole line is spoken. With a swift, salient, rising inflection on the opening word of the second line, an inflection which creates expectancy of change, the voice lifts the thought out of the minor into the major key. Because *pause* has no direct effect upon the voice, I have not before mentioned it, although it is a most vital element of vocal expression. But I must call your attention to its significance here by simply asking you to indulge in it. Stop after uttering the word "till" and study the effect of the pause. It is the pause quite as much as the inflection, you see, which induces the expectant attitude you desire to create in the mind of your auditor. With the next three words, "that May morn," the tone takes on a bit of the warmth of early summer. A lingering cadence on the word "May" will help the suggestion. With the third line the voice begins to shine. I know no other way to express it. The inflections are swift and straight, but not staccato, because they must suggest a growth, not a burst of color. The tone on which the words are borne must be continuous. It must not be broken off definitely with each word, as is to prove most effective, we shall find, in handling the third line of the second verse. The fourth line brings the full, glowing, radiant tone on the first word, "violets." This tone must be held in full volume on the last two words. The law for beautiful speech must be observed here. (But where should it not be observed?) Let us recall the law: "Beautiful speech depends upon openness of vowels and definiteness of consonants." The vowels give volume to a word, the consonants form. Slur your consonants and squeeze your vowels in the three words of this line, "Violets were born," and what becomes of this miracle of spring? The voicing of the second verse is very like that of the first. The opening line demands the same gray monotone. But the three words, "sky," "scowl," and "cloud," if clear-cut in utterance, as they should be, will break the level of the line more than the single word "starved" in the first line of the first verse can do, or was meant to do. There is the same swift lift of the voice in the opening word of the second line, the same change to the major key, the same growing glow in the tone on the third line, and the same radiant outburst of color sustained through the last line. The only difference lies in the suffusion of radiance in the tone to suggest the coming of color to the bank, in the first verse, and the outburst of radiance to suggest the sudden splitting of the clouds, and the star's swift birth, in the second verse. With the emotional change of thought in the last verse, from a travail and birth in nature, to a human soul's struggle and rebirth, the deepening color which creeps into the tone indicates the entrance of personal passion. The key does not change. The inflections are still and straight. The tone simply deepens and glows in the last two lines, as a prayerful ecstasy possesses the one who reads.

Mr. William James tells us that we learn to swim in winter and skate in summer. The principle underlying this statement is of immense comfort, as I have said, in approaching a class in vocal expression. The hope of satisfying results is fostered by the knowledge that a mere statement of the fundamental facts of right tone-production will do much toward inducing a right condition for tone. But I know, too, that immediate results depend upon immediate and faithful putting into practice of the principles set forth. A little practice every day will work swift wonders with the voice. And so, in leaving this phase of the training, I commend you to Ellen Terry's watchword, "infinite pains." When it means, as it does in pursuing this ideal, that we must be "on guard" every waking instant—*for a time;* when it means a watch set (for a time) upon every organ involved in expression—lips, teeth, tongue, jaw, mouth, throat, chest, diaphragm, and all the muscles governing these organs; when it means a watch set (for a time) upon one's every thought and emotion lest it make false demands upon the sensitive instruments of their expression—then it becomes a daring device, indeed, to wear upon

81

one's crest. Let us not hesitate to carve it there, when we realize that to follow it means culture, true culture, the culture which can only come through control and command of one's self.

PART III

STUDIES IN THE VOCAL INTERPRETATION OF LITERATURE

I

THE LAW OF APPROACH

WE turn now to a series of studies in vocal interpretation, based for convenience upon the analysis of various literary forms, beginning with the essay and the fable, passing through the lyric to the didactic poem, through the short story to the epic poem, and finally through the dramatic monologue to the play.

I have said that each of these forms makes its distinctive demand upon the voice of the interpreter. Before analyzing the particular form to determine the nature of that demand, let us consider the law of approach in entering upon the interpretation of any piece of literature, regardless of its form. Let us consider the relation of the reader to his text; and to his auditor. What should be my aim in reading aloud to you? Should it not be to convey to your mind as simply, clearly, and convincingly as possible the thought of the author? Yes, but I think the following statement of our relation is a little more comprehensive. As an interpreter of literature in any form, I must become a pure medium between the mind of the author and the mind of the auditor. In a final analysis I, the interpreter, must be a pure medium between life and your soul. I have said that the only excuse for the existence of a reader is that he should be an *interpreter*. I should have said *an interpreter of life through literature*. Let me illustrate. With a sense of protest, I had presented a play I loved, to an audience with which I felt little sympathy. By chance there was in that audience one of our best teachers and critics. After my recital I sought his criticism. Beginning, as the true critic always should, with a noting of some point of power, he said, "I congratulate you upon your illumined moments, but —they are too infrequent. You must multiply them." "What do you mean by my illumined moments?" I asked. "The moments when you do not get between your audience and the thought you are uttering— the moments when you become a revealer of life to them. Your attitude toward your audience is not sustained in the simplicity and clearness of some of its moments. You suddenly ring down the curtain in the middle of the scene. That spoils the scene, you know. You seem to feel a revolt against the giving of your confidence to the audience, and thereupon you immediately shut them away. You become conscious of yourself, and we, the audience, lose the vision and become conscious of you and the way you are reading or reciting or acting." Then he added, "Adelaide Neilson, at first, had illumined moments in her playing of Juliet, but finally her impersonation became one piece of illumination." That delightful teacher, reader, and critic, the late Mr. Howard Ticknor, suggested the same ideal in comparing a Juliet of to-day with Miss Neilson's Juliet. "When Miss ——— is on the balcony," he said, "you hear all around you: 'How lovely she looks! Isn't that robe dear? How beautiful her voice is!' When Miss Neilson lived that little minute, a breathless people prayed with Juliet, 'I would not for the world they found thee here,' and sighed with Romeo—'O blessed, blessed night! I am afeard, being in night, all this is but a dream.' Miss Neilson *was* Juliet. They, the audience, lived with these lovers one hour of lyric rapture, and could never again be quite so commonplace in their attitude toward the 'deathless passion.' They may not now remember Adelaide Neilson, but they remember that story, and forever carry a new vision of life and love, because the actress lost herself in the life of the play. She did not exploit her personality and let it stand between the audience and the drama." That is it: if we would be artists (and there is not one among us who would not be an artist) we must cease to put our little selves in front of our messages. In the home, in the office, in the houses of our friends, in the school-room, on the platform, on the stage, let us be *simple*, *natural*, *sincere*. Let us lay aside our mannerisms. Let us seek to know and reveal life. Then shall we be remembered: not, for a queer way of combing our hair, or lifting our eyes, or using our hands, or shrugging our shoulders; but for some revelation of truth or of beauty which we have brought to a community. When some one says to you — the reader or actress, "I shall never forget the way you raised your eyebrow at that point," don't stop to reply, but fly to your study and read the lines "at that point" over and over, with level brows, until you understand the meaning, and can express the thought so effectively by a lift of your voice that you no longer need the help of your eyebrow. Every gesture, every tone must call attention, not to itself, but to the hidden meaning of the author. It must illumine the text of the character portrayed. Then, with this attitude, which can only be described as *selfless*, let us enter upon our interpretative study of special forms.

I have said that each form makes its particular demand and appeal. If it is an essay that I am to read to you, the direct and fundamental appeal is to the mind; and the demand upon me, the reader, is for clear, concise thinking, revealed through unerring emphasis and definite, purposeful inflection. So read, it will inevitably persuade you to some readjustment of your ideas, your values, your discriminations; or it will strengthen you in convictions you already hold. If it is a fable that I am to interpret, the appeal is to the fancy; the demand upon my voice is for subtle lights and shades of tone and a mastery of swift changes in inflection. If read as a fable should be read, it will leave you less serious in your attitude toward your neighbor's harmless foibles and less critical of his failings. If it is a short story the demand upon me is for a sustained vitality of tone and temper, in order that I may carry you with unflagging interest through some new or old experience, and show you how to meet or how not to meet certain crises in life. If it is a lyric (sonnet, ballad, psalm, ode, or elegy) its fundamental appeal is to emotion; and its demand upon me is for a mastery of tone-color, a sense of rhythm, and the power to suggest a background of musical sound. So read, it will add to your power to forgive, pity, endure, forbear, understand, and love. If it is an epic poem, concerned with the deeds of heroes and heroines, its demand is for each and all of the qualities already noted. And a right interpretation, through a just use of these qualities, will add to your courage and skill and foresight. If it is a dramatic monologue a further demand is made upon me for character identification. I must lend myself to the spirit of the speaker. I must let him speak to you through me. If I present the monologue in the right spirit you will understand a certain type of person better. Finally, if it is a play that I am presenting I must identify myself not with one character, but with several. I must be so volatile in voice, body, and mind that the transition from character to character will not interrupt the movement of the play. If I present a drama thus powerfully it will make

91

you see more clearly the relations of men and events and give you a truer understanding of life.

In turning now to a particular study of the particular form, we must assume that we have mastered the first steps in vocal training: that our instruments are in tune and so ready for use; and that we have acquired a more or less efficient vocal vocabulary. We are now to use the tuned instrument and its acquired vocabulary in interpreting, first, the essay.

II

THE ESSAY

WHY do we choose the essay for our first study in vocal analysis? Because a fault fundamental to all other faults, in tone production and vocal expression, rises from a failure to think clearly. The appeal of the essay is primarily an intellectual appeal. It demands concentration of the mind upon its thought to make it your own; and clear and concise utterance of its phrases to convey that thought to another. To really grasp and adequately present a philosophical essay involves mental discipline similar to that required in solving a mathematical problem. I have taken my examples for analysis from Emerson, because Emerson's almost every paragraph is an essay in miniature. In printing extracts from this source we feel no sense of incompleteness. Let us read this passage from "Experience":

"To finish the moment, to find the journey's end in every step of the road, to live the greatest number of good hours, is wisdom. It is not the part of men, but of fanatics—or of mathematicians, if you will—to say that, the shortness of life considered, it is not worth caring whether for so short a duration we were sprawling in want or sitting high. Since our office is with moments, let us husband them. Five minutes of to-day are worth as much to me as five minutes in the next millennium. Let us be poised, and wise, and our own, to-day. I settle myself ever the firmer in the creed that we should not postpone and refer and wish, but do broad justice where we are, by whomsoever we deal with, accepting our actual companions and circumstances, however humble or odious, as the mystic officials to whom the universe has delegated its whole pleasure for us."

If you do not think your way through this paragraph clearly, concisely, logically, intensely, when you read it aloud your voice will betray you. In what way? Your tone will lack resonance, your speech will lack precision, your pitch will be monotonous, your touch will be uncertain, your inflections will be indefinite. Your reading will be unconvincing, because it will fail in lucidity and variety. In approaching this passage let us study first the question of proper emphasis. What is emphasis? The dictionaries tell us that, in delivery, it is a special stress of the voice on a given word. But we must use it in a broader sense than this. To emphasize a word is not merely to put a special stress of the voice upon that word. Such an attack might only make the word conspicuous and so defeat the aim of true emphasis. True emphasis is the art of voicing the words in a phrase so that they shall assume a right relation to each other and, so related, best suggest the thought of which they are the symbols. I do not emphasize one word in a phrase and not the others. I simply vary my stress upon each word, in order to gain the proper perspective for the whole sentence. Just so, in a picture, I make one object stand out, and others fall into the background, by drawing or painting them in proper relations to each other. I may use any or all of the "elements of vocal expression" to give that proper relation of values to the words in a single phrase. I may pause, change my pitch, vary my inflection, and alter my tone-color, in order to give a single word its full value. Let us try experiments in emphasis, with some isolated sentences, before analyzing the longer passage. Here is one of Robert Louis Stevenson's beautifully wrought periods, "Every man has a sane spot somewhere." Let us vary, vocally, the relative values of the words in this sentence, and study the effect upon the character of the thought. Let us look upon the statement as a theme for discussion. With a pause before the second word, "man," a lift of the voice on that word, a whimsical turn of the tone, and a significant inflection, we may convert an innocent statement of fact into an incendiary question for debate on the comparative sanity of the sexes. A plea for endless faith and charity becomes a back-handed criticism of women. Now let us read the sentence, giving it its true meaning. "Every man has a sane spot somewhere." Let your voice make of the statement a plea, by dwelling a bit on the first

word and again on the last word. Hyphen-
ate the first two words (they really stand
for one idea). Compound also the words
sane and *spot*. Lift them as a single word
above the rest of the sentence. Now put
somewhere a little higher still above the level
of the rest of the sentence. So, only, have
we the true import of this group of words:

          : some
                   where.
     sane-spot

Every-
      man has a

Analyze the rest of these sentences from
Stevenson in the same way, and experiment
with them vocally.

"That is never a bad wind that blows where we
want to go."

"For truth that is suppressed by friends is the
readiest weapon of the enemy."

"Some strand of our own misdoing is involved
in every quarrel."

"Drama is the poetry of conduct, romance the
poetry of circumstance."

"You cannot run away from a weakness; you must sometime fight it out or perish; and if that be so, why not now, and where you stand?"

"An aim in life is the only fortune worth the finding; and it is not to be found in foreign lands, but in the heart itself."

"The world was not made for us; it was made for ten hundred millions of me, all different 'from each other and from us; there's no royal road, we just have to sclamber and tumble."

Now, once more, and this time with detailed analysis, let us study the passage from "Experience." Let us first consider for a moment some of the words which make this passage powerful: *finish, journey's-end, good-hours, wisdom, fanatics, mathematicians, sprawling-in-want, sitting-high, firmer, poised, postpone, justice, humble, odious, mystic, pleasure.* When spoken with a keen sense of its inherent meaning, with full appreciation of its form, and with delight in moulding it, how efficient each one of these words becomes. When shall we, as a people, learn reverence for the words which make up our language—reverence that shall make us ashamed to mangle words, offering as our excuse that we are "Westerners" or "Southerners" or from New York or New England or Indiana. The clear-cut thought calls for the clean-cut speech. Let us say these words over and over until they assume full value. And now we pass from words to groups of words. The mind and the tone must move progressively through the first three phrases which make up this first sentence: "To finish the moment, to find the journey's end in every step of the road, to live the greatest number of good hours, is wisdom." The phrases must be held together by an almost imperceptible suspension and upward reach of the voice at the end of each group of words, and yet each phrase must be allowed to be momentarily complete. Read the sentence, making each phrase a conclusion, and then again letting each phrase look forward to the next. Each phrase is really a substantive, looking forward to its predicate through a second substantive which is a little more vital than the first, and again through a third substantive which is a little more vital than either of the other two. Bring this out in reading the sentence. The next sentence depends for its significance upon your contrasting inflections of the three words, *men*, *fanatics*, and *mathematicians;* and again upon your sympathetic inflection of *sprawling-in-want* and *sitting-high*. "It is not the part of men, but of fanatics—or of mathematicians, if you will—to say that, the shortness of life considered, it is not worth caring whether for so short a duration we were sprawling in want or sitting high." In your utterance of these words can you make "men" MEN, and "fanatics" *fanatics*, and consign "mathematicians" to the cold corner of human affairs designed for them? Can you so inflect "sprawling in want" and "sitting high " as to suggest a swamp and a mountain-top, or a frog and an angel? Let your voice leap from the swamp to the mountain - top. Let it climb. Now comes the swift, concise, admonitory sentence: "Since our office is with moments, let us husband them." Pause before you speak the word "husband," and *husband* it. "Five minutes of to-day are worth as much to me as five minutes in the next millennium." Make "five minutes of to-day" one word, and accent the last syllable, thus: five-minutes-of-*to-day*. Let the tone retard and take its time on the last seven words. Now poise your tone for the next sentence. "Let us be poised, and wise, and our own, to-day." The paragraph closes with a more complex statement of the theme. Let your voice search out the meaning. Let it settle down into the conclusion, and utter it convincingly. Give a definite touch to the words which I shall put in italics. "I settle myself ever *firmer* in the *creed* that we should not *postpone* and *refer* and *wish*, but do *broad-justice* where we *are*, *by whomsoever* we deal with, accepting our *actual* companions and circumstances, however *humble* or *odious*, as the *mystic officials* to whom the *universe* has dedicated its *whole pleasure* for *us*."

This is a suggestive analysis for the vocal interpretation of the essay. The examples which follow are for you to analyze in the

same way, but with your *voice in your study*
—not with a pencil on paper.

"There is a time in every man's education
when he arrives at the conviction that envy is
ignorance; that imitation is suicide; that he must
take himself for better for worse as his portion;
that though the wide universe is full of good, no
kernel of nourishing corn can come to him but
through his toil bestowed on that plot of ground
which is given to him to till.   The power which
resides in him is new in nature, and none but he
knows what that is which he can do, nor does he
know until he has tried. . . . What I must do is
all that concerns me, not what the people think.
This rule, equally arduous in actual and in intellectual life, may serve for the whole distinc-
tion between greatness and meanness. It is
the harder because you will always find those
who think they know what is your duty better
than you know it. It is easy in the world to
live after the world's opinion; it is easy in
solitude to live after our own; but the great man
is he who in the midst of the crowd keeps with
perfect sweetness the independence of solitude."
                              —*Self-Reliance*.

*   *   *   *   *   *

"Happy is the house that shelters a friend!
It might well be built, like a festal bower or

arch, to entertain him a single day. Happier,
if he know the solemnity of that relation and
honor its law! It is no idle bond, no holiday en-
gagement. He who offers himself a candidate
for that covenant comes up, like an Olympian,
to the great games where the first-born of the
world are the competitors. He proposes himself for contest where Time, Want, Danger, are
in the lists, and he alone is victor who has truth
enough in his constitution to preserve the
delicacy of his beauty from the wear and tear
of all these. The gifts of fortune may be present
or absent, but all the hap in that contest depends on intrinsic nobleness and the contempt
of trifles. There are two elements that go to
the composition of friendship, each so sovereign
that I can detect no superiority in either, no
reason why either should be first named. One
is Truth. A friend is a person with whom I
may be sincere. Before him I may think
aloud. . . . The other element of friendship is
Tenderness. We are holden to men by every
sort of tie, by blood, by pride, by fear, by hope,
by lucre, by lust, by hate, by admiration, by
every circumstance and badge and trifle, but
we can scarce believe that so much character
can subsist in another as to draw us by love.
Can another be so blessed and we so pure that
we can offer him tenderness? When a man be-

comes dear to me I have touched the goal of fortune."—*Friendship*.

*   *   *   *   *   *

"A gentleman makes no noise: a lady is serene. ... The person who screams, or uses the superlative degree, or converses with heat, puts whole drawing-rooms to flight. If you wish to be loved, love measure."—*Manners*.

*   *   *   *   *   *

"The reason why we feel one man's presence, and do not feel another's, is as simple as gravity. Truth is the summit of being: justice is the application of it to affairs. All individual natures stand in a scale, according to the purity of this element in them. The will of the pure runs down from them into other natures, as water runs down from a higher into a lower vessel. This natural force is no more to be withstood than any other natural force. We can drive a stone upward for a moment into the air, but it is yet true that all stones will forever fall; and whatever instances can be quoted of unpunished theft, or of a lie which somebody credited, justice must prevail, and it is the privilege of truth to make itself believed. Character is this moral order seen through the medium of an individual nature. An individual

104

is an encloser. Time and space, liberty and necessity, truth and thought, are left at large no longer. Now, the universe is a close or pound. All things exist in the man tinged with the manners of his soul. . . . A healthy soul stands united with the Just and the True, as the magnet arranges itself with the pole, so that he stands to all beholders like a transparent object betwixt them and the sun, and whoso journeys toward the sun, journeys toward that person. He is thus the medium of the highest influence to all who are not on the same level. Thus men of character are the conscience of the society to which they belong."—*Character*.

In proposing further material for use in establishing this step in vocal interpretation, I shall make a suggestion to the public-school teacher of the work only. The problem here is simpler than it seems to be at first. Let the student bring to his class in Expression his text-book in any other subject, preferably Nature Study, Science, or History. Three things can be accomplished by this plan: The history or science lesson will be mastered in half the time it might otherwise take; a right habit of study will be established; and the first step in learning to read aloud will be accomplished. This solves the much-vexed question of a text-book in reading, for the time at least.

III

THE FABLE

IN turning, in our interpretative study, from the essay to the lyric, let us pause for a moment and seek relaxation with the fable. Do you not agree with me that the reading of the fable, whether to children or "grown-ups," should be a bit whimsical in tone? Perhaps I only mean that I should choose to have my "whimsical friend" read fables and fairy-stories to me. What is a fable? "A story in which, by the imagined dealings of men with animals or mere things, or by the supposed doings of these alone, useful lessons are taught." It is the presence of the *lesson* that must be offset by the whimsical tone. A moral "rubbed in" is like an overdose of certain kinds of medicine. A little cures, too much may kill. I print for your use at this point three of Æsop's fables.

THE LION AND THE MOUSE

Once when a lion was asleep a little mouse began running up and down upon him; this soon wakened the lion, who placed his huge paw upon him, and opened his big jaws to swallow him. "Pardon, O King," cried the little mouse; "forgive me this time. I shall never forget it: who knows but what I may be able to do you a turn some of these days?" The lion was so tickled at the idea of the mouse being able to help him, that he lifted up his paw and let him go. Some time after the lion was caught in a trap, and the hunters, who desired to carry him alive to the king, tied him to a tree while they went in search of a wagon to carry him on. Just then the little mouse happened to pass by, and seeing the sad plight in which the lion was, went up to him and soon gnawed away the ropes that bound the king of the beasts. "Was I not right?" said the little mouse.

"Little friends may prove great friends."

THE WIND AND THE SUN

The wind and the sun were disputing which was the stronger. Suddenly they saw a traveller coming down the road, and the sun said: "I see a way to decide our dispute. Whichever of us can cause that traveller to take off his cloak shall be regarded as the stronger. You begin." So the sun retired behind a cloud, and the wind began to blow as hard as he could upon the traveller. But the harder he blew the more closely did the traveller wrap his cloak round him, till at last the wind had to give up in despair. Then the sun came out and shone in all his glory upon the traveller, who soon found it too hot to walk with his cloak on.

"Kindness effects more than severity."

THE CROW AND THE PITCHER

A crow, half dead with thirst, came upon a pitcher which had once been full of water; but when the crow put his beak into the mouth of the pitcher he found that only very little water was left in it, and that he could not reach far enough down to get at it. He tried, and he tried, but at last had to give up in despair. Then a thought came to him, and he took a pebble and dropped it into the pitcher. Then he took another pebble and dropped it into the pitcher. Then he took another pebble and dropped that into the pitcher. Then he took another pebble and dropped that into the pitcher. Then he took another pebble and dropped that into the pitcher. Then he took another pebble and dropped that into the pitcher. At last, at last, he saw the water mount up near him; and after casting in a few more pebbles he was able to quench his thirst and save his life.

"Little by little does the trick."

I shall not analyze these fables for you. You can hardly fail in right use of emphasis. Your only danger lies in making your touch too heavy. Let me speak of one point in the fable of "The Crow and the Pitcher." How shall we avoid monotony in reading the lines beginning, "Then he took another pebble and dropped it into the pitcher"? This line is followed by one in which but two words are changed, and then by a line with but one change, and then by three lines with no change at all We must depend upon varying the emphasis and movement. Try this treatment: Give "another" the particular stress in reading the first line. Pause at the close of the line as if to study the effect of the pebble. In the next line "that," of course, takes the emphasis. Pause before the word and give it a salient stress. The movement of the voice through these two lines has been deliberate. On the next line hasten it a little, and make the pause at the close of the line shorter. With the fourth line, let the tone settle down to work. Give each of the first five words equal stress. With the fifth and last line let us feel that you may "go on forever," and surprise us with a very short pause and a joyful stress upon "at last, at last," and don't fail to let the enthusiasm of your tone give us the full sense of relief which comes with the mounting of the water; and the delight in the conclusion —"he was able to quench his thirst and save his life." And now, most whimsically, let us voice the moral, "Little by little does the trick."

IV

LYRIC POETRY

WE turn now in our study, from didactic prose to lyric poetry. We do so because the direct appeal of a lyric poem is to the emotions. The nature of the demand upon the interpreter changes. And new power is developed along new lines. While literature, whatever its form, must compel the reader's thought, its predominant appeal in poetry must be to emotion. In our study of technique we learned that tone-color was the vocal language of emotion. So the vocal interpretation of poetry (whether lyric, pastoral, or didactic) demands, above all, a mastery of this element of our vocabulary. The reading of poetry also demands a sense of rhythm, metre, and rhyme. Can this sense be developed? Yes! It should be a part of

the training of every child's soul.   How can
it be accomplished?   Read poetry to him
and with him.

We shall take for our study of the lyric
Shelley's ode, "To a Skylark."   I shall analyze in detail only the first five stanzas:

> "Hail to thee, blithe Spirit!
>   Bird thou never wert,
> That from heaven, or near it
>   Pourest thy full heart
> In profuse strains of unpremeditated art.
>
> "Higher still and higher
>   From the earth thou springest,
> Like a cloud of fire,
>   The blue deep thou wingest,
> And singing still dost soar, and soaring ever singest.
>
> "In the golden lightning
>   Of the sunken sun
> O'er which clouds are brightening,
>   Thou dost float and run,
> Like an unbodied joy whose race is just begun.
>
> "The pale purple even
>   Melts around thy flight;
> Like a star of heaven
>   In the broad daylight
> Thou art unseen, but yet I hear thy shrill delight.

113

THE SPEAKING VOICE

"Keen as are the arrows
Of that silver sphere
Whose intense lamp narrows
In the white dawn clear,
Until we hardly see, we feel that it is there."

How shall we create an atmosphere for the reading of these verses! How can we catch the spirit of the creator of them! Shall we ever feel ready to voice that first line? Do you know Jules Breton's picture, "The Lark"? Do you love it? Go, then, and stand before it for an hour, actually or in imagination. Something of the spirit which informs that lovely child, lifting her eyes, her head in an attitude of listening rapture, must steal over you as you stand before her. I know her power. I have tested it. In reading the "Skylark" with a class of boys and girls from twelve to fourteen years old, I tried the experiment. I happened to have with me a beautiful copy of Breton's picture. I took it to the class-room. I wrote on the blackboard verses of the poem and hung the picture over them. The *picture* taught them to read the poem. The eyes of the girl became their teacher. I tried the experiment, with a private pupil in my studio, with a somewhat different result. I had told her to bring a copy of Shelley's poems to her next lesson. "Do you know the ode 'To a Skylark'?" I asked. "Yes," she said. A copy of Breton's picture hung on the wall. "Before you open your book, look at the picture," I said. She obeyed. Her expression, always radiant, deepened its radiance. "Do you know what the girl is doing?" I asked. "Oh yes, she is listening to the skylark." "How do you know?" "I have heard the skylark sing." "I never have," I said. "Read the poem to me." Now when *I* read the "Skylark," I see the girl in Jules Breton's picture, but I hear the voice of my English pupil.

But if our apperceptive background fails to furnish a memory of the identical sight and sound for our inspiring, it at least holds bird notes and bird flights of great beauty, and we must call upon these for the impulse to voice Shelley's apostrophe:

115

THE SPEAKING VOICE

"Hail to thee, blithe Spirit!
Bird thou never wert,
That from heaved, or near it
Pourest thy full heart
In profuse strains of unpremeditated art."

An early autumn number of the *Atlantic Monthly* for 1907 published a poem by Mr. Ridgley Torrence, entitled "The Lesser Children," or " A Threnody at the Hunting Season." The poem is worthy, in sentiment and structure, to be set beside Shelley's ode. Let us compare with the picture which the eighteenth - century poet has given us, this one from our modern song-writer:

"Who has not seen in the high gulf of light
What, lower, was a bird, but now
Is moored and altered quite
Into an island of unshaded joy?
To whom the mate below upon the bough
Shouts once and brings him from his high employ.
Yet speeding he forgot not of the cloud
Where he from glory sprang and burned aloud,
But took a little of the day,
A little of the colored sky,
And of the joy that would not stay
He wove a song that cannot die."

Now let us study closely the first verse
of the older poem. Spirit and voice must
soar in the first line, "Hail to thee, blithe
Spirit!" The two words "hail" and "blithe"
are swift-winged words. Let them fly. Give
them their wings. Let them do all they are
intended to do. The rhythm of the whole
poem is aspiring. Reverence the rhythm,
but keep the thought floating clear above it
in the second line, "Bird thou never wert."
With the next two lines the tone must gather
head to be poured forth in the last line, "In
profuse strains of unpremeditated art." Let
us make another comparative study. Set on
the other side of this picture Lowell's de-
scription of the "little bird" in his prologue
to Sir Launfal's vision:

"The little bird sits at his door in the sun,
   Atilt like a blossom among the leaves,
And lets his illumined being o'errun
   With the deluge of summer it receives."

The second verse of the "Skylark" demands a still higher flight of imagination and
tone. Let us try it.

THE SPEAKING VOICE

"Higher still and higher
From the earth thou springest,
Like a cloud of fire
The blue deep thou wingest,
And singing still dost soar, and soaring ever singest."

Again all the words rise and float. Sing them over: *higher, higher, springest, fire, wingest, singing, soar, soaring, singest.* The reader must feel himself poised for flight in every word of the first three verses. Why does the poet say cloud of fire? What is the color of the skylark? And now the tone, which has been of a radiant hue through these three verses, must soften a little in the first three lines of the next verse—

"The pale purple even
Melts around thy flight";—

glow gold again in the last three lines—

"Like a star of heaven
In the broad daylight
Thou art unseen, and yet I hear thy shrill delight"—

and become the white of an incandescent light in the next verse—

"Keen as are the arrows
Of that silver sphere
Whose intense lamp narrows
In the white dawn clear,
Until we hardly see, we feel that it is there."

Do you not see that the secret of its beauty lies, for vocal interpretation, in the color of tone and in the inflection of the words?   Say "unseen," dwelling on the second syllable; "shrill delight," directing *shrill* over the head of *delight;* "keen," making it cleave the air like an arrow; "silver sphere," suggesting a moonlit path across water; "intense" and "narrows," letting the tone recede into the "white dawn"; "see," with a vanishing stress; and "feel," with a deepening note carried to the end.   So we might go on through the twenty-one stanzas which make up the poem.

Please analyze undirected the next two verses.

"All the earth and air
With thy voice is loud,
As, when night is bare,
From one lonely cloud
The moon rains out her beams, and heaven is overflow'd.

THE SPEAKING VOICE

"What thou art we know not;
  What is most like thee?
From rainbow clouds there flow not
  Drops so bright to see
As from thy presence showers a rain of melody."

In reading the first lines of the next four verses we must avoid monotony.

"Like a poet hidden
  In the light of thought,
Singing hymns unbidden,
  Till the world is wrought
To sympathy with hopes and fears it heeded not:

"Like a high-born maiden
  In a palace tower,
Soothing her love-laden
  Soul in secret hour
With music sweet as love, which overflows her bower:

"Like a glowworm golden
  In a dell of dew,
Scattering unbeholden
  Its aerial hue
Among the flowers and grass, which screen it from
  the view:

"Like a rose embower'd
  In its own green leaves,
By warm winds deflower'd,
  Till the scent it gives
Makes faint with too much sweet these heavy-
  wingèd thieves."

LYRIC POETRY

Vary, if only for variety, the pitch on
which you begin each of these first lines.
Let the first three words of the eighth verse,
"like a poet," ascend in pitch. Keep the
voice level in the first line of the ninth verse,
"like a high-born maiden." Let the pitch
fall in the first words of the tenth stanza,
"like a glowworm golden." And again keep
the tone level on the first line of the next
stanza, "like a rose embower'd." I leave to
you the analysis of the rest of the poem:

"Sound of vernal showers
    On the twinkling grass,
Rain-awaken'd flowers,
    All that ever was
Joyous, and clear, and fresh, thy music doth sur-
    pass.

"Teach us, sprite or bird,
    What sweet thoughts are thine:
I have never heard
    Praise of love or wine
That panted forth a flood of rapture so divine.

"Chorus hymeneal
    Or triumphal chaunt
Match'd with thine, would be all
    But an empty vaunt—
A thing wherein we feel there is some hidden want.

121

THE SPEAKING VOICE

"What objects are the fountains
  Of thy happy strain?
What field, or waves, or mountains?
  What shapes of sky or plain?
What love of thine own kind? what ignorance of
  pain?

"With thy clear, keen joyance
  Languor cannot be:
Shadow of annoyance
  Never came near thee:
Thou lovest; but ne'er knew love's sad satiety.

"Waking or asleep
  Thou of death must deem
Things more true and deep
  Than we mortals dream,
Or how could thy notes flow in such a crystal
  stream?

"We look before and after,
  And pine for what is not:
Our sincerest laughter
  With some pain is fraught;
Our sweetest songs are those that tell of saddest
  thought.

"Yet if we could scorn
  Hate and pride and fear;
If we were things born
  Not to shed a tear,
I know not how thy joy we ever should come hear.

LYRIC POETRY

"Better than all measures
  Of delightful sound,
Better than all treasures
  That in books are found,
Thy skill to poet were, thou scorner of the ground!

"Teach me half the gladness
  That thy brain must know,
Such harmonious madness
  From my lips would flow,
The world should listen then, as I am listening
  now!"   —P. B. SHELLEY.

The following selections from lyric poetry are designed to give your voice exercise in the expression of varied emotions. I understand that Dr. Curry makes the reading of joyous lyrics an important part of his voice programme.

HUNTING SONG

"Waken, lords and ladies gay,
  On the mountain dawns the day;
All the jolly chase is here
  With hawk and horse and hunting-spear;
Hounds are in their couples yelling,
Hawks are whistling, horns are knelling,
Merrily, merrily mingle they,
'Waken, lords and ladies gay.'

123

THE SPEAKING VOICE

"Waken, lords and ladies gay,
  The mist has left the mountain gray,
  Springlets in the dawn are steaming,
  Diamonds on the brake are gleaming;
  And foresters have busy been
  To track the buck in thicket green;
  Now we come to chant our lay
  'Waken, lords and ladies gay.'

"Waken, lords and ladies gay,
  To the greenwood haste away;
  We can show you where he lies,
  Fleet of foot and tall of size;
  We can show the marks he made
  When 'gainst the oak his antlers fray'd;
  You shall see him brought to bay;
  'Waken, lords and ladies gay.'

"Louder, louder chant the lay
  Waken, lords and ladies gay!
  Tell them youth and mirth and glee
  Run a course as well as we;
  Time, stern huntsman! who can baulk,
  Stanch as hound and fleet as hawk;
  Think of this, and rise with day,
  Gentle lords and ladies gay!"
                  —Sir W. Scott.

"It was a lover and his lass
  With a hey and a ho, and a hey nonino!
  That o'er the green cornfield did pass

In the spring-time, the only pretty ring time,
When birds do sing hey ding a ding:
  Sweet lovers love the Spring.

"Between the acres of the rye
These pretty country folks would lie:
This carol they began that hour,
How, that life was but a flower:

"And therefore take the present time
  With a hey and a ho and a hey nonino!
For love is crownèd with the prime
In spring-time, the only pretty ring time,
When birds do sing hey ding a ding:
  Sweet lovers love the Spring."
              —W. Shakespeare.

"Pack, clouds, away, and welcome day,
  With night we banish sorrow;
Sweet air blow soft, mount larks aloft
  To give my Love good-morrow!
Wings from the wind to please her mind
  Notes from the lark I'll borrow;
Bird, prune thy wing, nightingale sing,
  To give my Love good-morrow;
    To give my Love good-morrow
    Notes from them both I'll borrow.

"Wake from thy nest, Robin-redbreast,
  Sing, birds, in every furrow;
And from each hill, let music shrill
  Give my fair Love good-morrow!

THE SPEAKING VOICE

Blackbird and thrush in every bush,
Stare, linnet, and cock-sparrow!
You pretty elves, among yourselves
Sing my fair Love good-morrow;
To give my Love good-morrow
Sing, birds, in every furrow!"
—T. HEYWOOD.

MEMORY [1]

"My mind lets go a thousand things,
Like dates of wars and deaths of kings,
And yet recalls the very hour—
'Twas noon by yonder village tower,
And on the last blue noon in May—
The wind came briskly up this way,
Crisping the brook beside the road;
Then, pausing here, set down its load
Of pine-scents, and shook listlessly
Two petals from that wild-rose-tree."

ENAMOURED ARCHITECT OF AIRY RHYME

"Enamoured architect of airy rhyme,
Build as thou wilt; heed not what each man
says:
Good souls, but innocent of dreamer's ways,
Will come, and marvel why thou wastest time;
Others, beholding how thy turrets climb

[1] This and the following poem appear by special permission of Houghton, Mifflin Co., the publishers of Mr. Aldrich's poems.

'Twixt theirs and heaven, will hate thee all thy
　　days;
But most beware of those who come to praise.
O Wondersmith, O Worker in sublime
And Heaven-sent dreams, let art be all in all;
　　Build as thou wilt, unspoiled by praise or blame,
　　　Build as thou wilt, and as thy light is given:
Then, if at last the airy structure fall,
　　Dissolve, and vanish—take thyself no shame.
　　　They fail, and they alone, who have not striven."
　　　　　　—THOMAS BAILEY ALDRICH.

LOVE IN THE WINDS [1]

" When I am standing on a mountain crest,
　　Or hold the tiller in the dashing spray,
My love of you leaps foaming in my breast,
　　Shouts with the winds and sweeps to their foray;
My heart bounds with the horses of the sea,
　　And plunges in the wild ride of the night,
Flaunts in the teeth of tempest the large glee
　　That rides out Fate and welcomes gods to fight.
Ho, love, I laugh aloud for love of you,
　　Glad that our love is fellow to rough weather,—
No fretful orchid hot-housed from the dew,
　　But hale and hardy as the highland heather,
Rejoicing in the wind that stings and thrills,
Comrades of ocean, playmate of the hills."
　　　　　　—RICHARD HOVEY.

[1] From " Along the Trail," by Richard Hovey.
Copyright, 1898, by Small, Maynard, & Co., Duffield &
Company, successors.

127

THE SPEAKING VOICE

CANDLEMAS[1]

"O hearken, all ye little weeds
 That lie beneath the snow,
  (So low, dear hearts, in poverty so low!)
The sun hath risen for royal deeds,
A valiant wind the vanguard leads;
Now quicken ye, lest unborn seeds
 Before ye rise and blow.

"O furry living things, adream
 On Winter's drowsy breast,
  (How rest ye there, how softly, safely rest!)
Arise and follow where a gleam
Of wizard gold unbinds the stream,
And all the woodland windings seem
 With sweet expectance blest.

"My birds, come back! the hollow sky
 Is weary for your note.
  (Sweet-throat, come back! O liquid, mellow
   throat!)
Ere May's soft minions hereward fly,
Shame on ye, laggards, to deny
The brooding breast, the sun-bright eye,
 The tawny, shining coat!"
       —ALICE BROWN.

"She was a Phantom of delight
 When first she gleam'd upon my sight;
 A lovely Apparition, sent
 To be a moment's ornament;

[1] By permission of Houghton, Mifflin Co.

128

LYRIC POETRY

Her eyes as stars of twilight fair;
Like Twilight's, too, her dusky hair;
But all things else about her drawn;
From May-time and the cheerful dawn;
A dancing shape, an image gay,
To haunt, to startle, and waylay.

"I saw her upon nearer view,
A Spirit, yet a Woman too!
Her household motions light and free,
And steps of virgin-liberty;
A countenance in which did meet
Sweet records, promises as sweet;
A creature not too bright or good
For human nature's daily food,
For transient sorrows, simple wiles,
Praise, blame, love, kisses, tears, and smiles.

"And now I see with eye serene
The very pulse of the machine;
A being breathing thoughtful breath,
A traveller between life and death:
The reason firm, the temperate will,
Endurance, foresight, strength, and skill;
A perfect Woman, nobly plann'd
To warn, to comfort, and command;
And yet a Spirit still, and bright
With something of an angel-light."
                                    —W. WORDSWORTH.

THE SPEAKING VOICE

NONSENSE LYRICS

TOPSY-TURVY WORLD

If the butterfly courted the bee,
  And the owl the porcupine;
If churches were built in the sea,
  And three times one was nine;
If the pony rode his master,
  If the buttercups ate the cows,
If the cats had the dire disaster
  To be worried, sir, by the mouse;
If mamma, sir, sold the baby
  To a gypsy for half a crown;
If a gentleman, sir, was a lady,
  The world would be Upside-down!
If any or all of these wonders
  Should ever come about,
I should not consider them blunders,
  For I should be inside-out!

CHORUS

  Ba-ba black wool,
    Have you any sheep?
  Yes, sir, a pack full.
    Creep, mouse, creep!
  Four-and-twenty little maids
    Hanging out the pie,
  Out jump'd the honey-pot,
    Guy Fawkes, Guy!

Cross latch, cross latch.
  Sit and spin the fire;
When the pie was open'd,
  The bird was on the brier!
          —WILLIAM BRIGHTY RANDS.

I SAW A NEW WORLD

I saw a new world in my dream,
Where all the folks alike did seem:
There was no Child, there was no Mother,
There was no Change, there was no Other.

For everything was Same, the Same;
There was no praise, there was no blame;
There was neither Need nor Help for it;
There was nothing fitting or unfit.

Nobody laugh'd, nobody wept;
None grew weary, so none slept;
There was nobody born, and nobody wed;
This world was a world of the living-dead.

I long'd to hear the Time-Clock strike
In the world where people were all alike;
I hated Same, I hated Forever;
I long'd to say Neither, or even Never.

I long'd to mend, I long'd to make;
I long'd to give, I long'd to take;

THE SPEAKING VOICE

I long'd for a change, whatever came after,
I long'd for crying, I long'd for laughter.

At last I heard the Time-Clock boom,
And woke from my dream in my little room;
With a smile on her lips my Mother was nigh,
And I heard the baby crow and cry.

And I thought to myself, How nice it is
For me to live in a world like this,
Where things can happen, and clocks can strike,
And none of the people are made alike;

Where Love wants this, and Pain wants that,
Where all our hearts want Tit for Tat
In the jumbles we make with our heads and our
    hands,
In a world that nobody understands,

But with work and hope, and the right to call
Upon Him who sees it and knows us all!
                    —WILLIAM BRIGHTY RANDS.

Besides the rivers, Arve and Arveiron, which
have their sources in the foot of Mount Blanc,
five conspicuous torrents rush down its sides;
and within a few paces of the Glaciers, the
Gentiana Major grows in immense numbers,
with its "flowers of loveliest blue."

HYMN

BEFORE SUNRISE, IN THE VALE OF CHAMOUNI

"Hast thou a charm to stay the morning-star
In his steep course? So long he seems to pause
On thy bald awful head, O sovran Blanc!
The Arve and Arveiron at thy base
Rave ceaselessly; but thou, most awful Form!
Risest from forth thy silent sea of pines,
How silently! Around thee and above
Deep is the air and dark, substantial, black,
An ebon mass: methinks thou piercest it,
As with a wedge! But when I look again,
It is thine own calm home, thy crystal shrine,
Thy habitation from eternity!
O dread and silent Mount! I gazed upon thee,
Till thou, still present to the bodily sense,
Didst vanish from my thought: entranced in prayer
I worshipped the Invisible alone.

Yet, like some sweet beguiling melody,
So sweet, we know not we are listening to it,
Thou, the meanwhile, wast blending with my
        thought,
Yea, with my life and life's own secret joy:
Till the dilating Soul, enrapt, transfused,
Into the mighty vision passing—there
As in her natural form, swelled vast to Heaven!

Awake, my Soul! not only passive praise
Thou owest! not alone these swelling tears,
Mute thanks and secret ecstasy! Awake,
Voice of sweet song! Awake, my Heart, awake!
Green vales and icy cliffs, all join my Hymn.

133

THE SPEAKING VOICE

Thou first and chief, sole sovran of the Vale!
O struggling with the darkness all the night,
And visited all night by troops of stars,
Or when they climb the sky or when they sink;
Companion of the morning-star at dawn,
Thyself Earth's rosy star, and of the dawn
Co-herald: wake, O wake, and utter praise!
Who sank thy sunless pillars deep in Earth?
Who filled thy countenance with rosy light?
Who made thee parent of perpetual streams?

And you, ye five wild torrents fiercely glad!
Who called you forth from night and utter death,
From dark and icy caverns called you forth,
Down those precipitous, black, jagged Rocks,
Forever shattered and the same forever?

Who gave you your invulnerable life,
Your strength, your speed, your fury, and your
        joy,
Unceasing thunder and eternal foam?
And who commanded (and the silence came),
Here let the billows stiffen, and have rest?

Ye ice-falls! ye that from the mountain's brow
Adown enormous ravines slope amain—
Torrents, methinks, that heard a mighty voice,
And stopped at once amid their maddest plunge!
Motionless torrents! silent cataracts!
Who made you glorious as the gates of Heaven
Beneath the keen full moon? Who bade the Sun
Clothe you with rainbows? Who, with living
        flowers

Of loveliest blue, spread garlands at your feet?—
God! let the torrents, like a shout of nations,
Answer! and let the ice-plains echo, God!
God! sing ye meadow - streams with gladsome
    voice!
Ye pine - groves, with your soft and soul - like
    sounds!
And they too have a voice, yon piles of snow,
And in their perilous fall shall thunder, God!

Ye living flowers that skirt the eternal frost!
Ye wild goats sporting round the eagle's nest!
Ye eagles, play-mates of the mountain-storm!
Ye lightnings, the dread arrows of the clouds!
Ye signs and wonders of the element!
Utter forth God, and fill the hills with praise!

Thou too, hoar Mount! with thy sky-pointing
    peaks,
Oft from whose feet the avalanche, unheard,
Shoots downward, glittering through the pure
    serene
Into the depth of clouds that veil thy breast—
Thou too again—stupendous Mountain! thou
That as I raise my head, awhile bowed low
In adoration, upward from thy base
Slow travelling with dim eyes suffused with tears,
Solemnly seemest like a vapory cloud,
To rise before me—Rise, O ever rise,
Rise like a cloud of incense, from the Earth!
Thou kingly Spirit throned among the hills,
Thou dread ambassador from Earth to Heaven,
Great hierarch! tell thou the silent sky,

THE SPEAKING VOICE

And tell the stars, and tell yon rising sun,
Earth, with her thousand voices, praises God."
            —SAMUEL TAYLOR COLERIDGE.

JAUN'S SONG FROM "THE SPANISH GYPSY"

I

" Memory,
  Tell to me
  What is fair
  Past compare
    In the land of Tubal?

  Is it Spring's
  Lovely things,
  Blossoms white,
  Rosy dight?
    Then it is Pepita.

  Summer's crest
  Red-gold tressed,
    Corn-flowers peeping under?
  Idle noons,
  Lingering moons,
  Sudden cloud,
  Lightning's shroud,
  Sudden rain,
  Quick again
    Smiles where late was thunder?
  Are all these
  Made to please?
    So too is Pepita.

136

Autumn's prime,
Apple-time,
Smooth cheek round,
Heart all sound?—
Is it this
You would kiss?
   Then it is Pepita.

You can bring
No sweet thing,
But my mind
Still shall find
   It is my Pepita.

Memory
Says to me
It is she—
She is fair
Past compare
   In the land of Tubal."

PABLO'S SONG FROM "THE SPANISH GYPSY"

I

"Spring comes hither,
  Buds the rose;
Roses wither,
  Sweet spring goes.
    Ojalá, would she carry me!

137

THE SPEAKING VOICE

Summer soars—
  Wide-winged day,
White light pours,
  Flies away.
    Ojalá, would he carry me!

Soft winds blow,
  Westward born,
Onward go
  Toward the morn.
    Ojalá, would they carry me!

Sweet birds sing
  O'er the graves,
Then take wing
  O'er the waves.
    Ojalá, would they carry me!"
          —GEORGE ELIOT.

Mr. Gilbert Chesterton tells us that the real Robert Browning of literary history arrived with the Dramatic Lyrics. "In Dramatic Lyrics," says Mr. Chesterton, "Browning discovered the one thing that he could really do better than any one else— the dramatic lyric. The form is absolutely original: he had discovered a new field of

138

poetry, and in the centre of that field he had found himself." The form is new, but it obeys the fundamental law of lyric poetry, and so in our study belongs to this chapter. The new element which the word "dramatic" suggests makes a new and a somewhat broader demand upon the interpreter; therefore I have chosen this group of Dramatic Lyrics from Browning as the material for your final study of this form:

MY STAR

" All that I know
   Of a certain star
Is, it can throw
   (Like the angled spar)
Now a dart of red,
   Now a dart of blue;
Till my friends have said
   They would fain see, too,
   My star that dartles the red and the blue!
Then it stops like a bird; like a flower, hangs furled:
   They must solace themselves with the Saturn
      above it.
What matter to me if their star is a world?
   Mine has opened its soul to me; therefore I
      love it."

THE SPEAKING VOICE

CAVALIER TUNES

MARCHING ALONG

I

" Kentish Sir Byng stood for his King,
  Bidding the crop-headed Parliament swing:
  And, pressing a troop unable to stoop
  And see the rogues flourish and honest folk droop,
  Marched them along, fifty-score strong,
  Great-hearted gentlemen, singing this song.

· II

  God for King Charles! Pym and such carles
  To the Devil that prompts 'em their treasonous
      parles!
  Cavaliers, up! Lips from the cup,
  Hands from the pasty, nor bite take nor sup
  Till you're—
  *(Chorus) Marching along, fifty-score strong,
      Great-hearted gentlemen, singing this song.*

III

  Hampden to hell, and his obsequies' knell
  Serve Hazelrig, Fiennes, and young Harry as well!
  England, good cheer! Rupert is near!
  Kentish and loyalists, keep we not here,

  *(Chorus) Marching along, fifty-score strong,
      Great-hearted gentlemen, singing this song?*

LYRIC POETRY

IV

Then, God for King Charles! Pym and his snarls
To the Devil that pricks on such pestilent carles!
Hold by the right, you double your might;
So, onward to Nottingham, fresh for the fight. ·
(*Chorus*) *March we along, fifty-score strong,*
Great-hearted gentlemen, singing this song!"

GARDEN FANCIES

THE FLOWER'S NAME

I

" Here's the garden she walked across,
  Arm in my arm, such a short while since.
Hark, now I push its wicket, the moss
  Hinders the hinges and makes them wince!
She must have reached this shrub ere she turned,
  As back with that murmur the wicket swung;
For she laid the poor snail, my chance foot
    spurned,
  To feed and forget it the leaves among.

II

Down this side of the gravel walk
  She went while her robe's edge brushed the box:
And here she paused in her gracious talk
  To point me a moth on the milk-white phlox.

10   141

THE SPEAKING VOICE

Roses, ranged in valiant row,
  I will never think that she passed you by!
She loves you noble roses, I know;
  But yonder, see, where the rock-plants lie!

III

This flower she stopped at, finger on lip,
  Stooped over, in doubt, as settling its claim;
Till she gave me, with pride to make no slip,
  Its soft meandering Spanish name.
What a name! Was it love or praise?
  Speech half-asleep or song half-awake?
I must learn Spanish, one of these days,
  Only for that slow sweet name's sake.

IV

Roses, if I live and do well,
  I may bring her, one of these days,
To fix you fast with as fine a spell,
  Fit you each with his Spanish phrase;
But do not detain me now; for she lingers
  There, like sunshine over the ground,
And ever I see her soft white fingers
  Searching after the bud she found.

V

Flower, you Spaniard, look that you grow not,
  Stay as you are and be loved forever!
Bud, if I kiss you 'tis that you blow not:
  Mind, the shut pink mouth opens never!

For while it pouts, her fingers wrestle,
  Twinkling the audacious leaves between,
Till round they turn and down they nestle—
  Is not the dear mark still to be seen?

VI

Where I find her not, beauties vanish;
  Whither I follow her, beauties flee;
Is there no method to tell her in Spanish
  June's twice June since she breathed it with
      me?
Come, bud, show me the least of her traces,
  Treasure my lady's lightest footfall!
—Ah, you may flout and turn up your faces—
  Roses, you are not so fair after all!"
                —ROBERT BROWNING.

V

DIDACTIC POETRY

IF our study of didactic prose and lyric poetry has been faithful we shall have learned to think more vividly and to feel more intelligently. We shall also find that our speech has gained precision and that our tone has gained purity and power.

I shall ask you to test your own increase in power along any of these lines by a self-directed study of didactic poetry. I give you the didactic poem because it makes a double appeal: through its form to emotion; through its aim to the mind. I have given you examples of this form in which the beauty and fascination of metre, rhythm, and rhyme and the didactic nature of the thought do not seem to overbalance each other. If either one should predominate, you must, by your interpretation, strike the balance. In reading Robert Browning's "Rabbi Ben Ezra" (from which I shall quote but a few verses) you must carry to your auditor the full import of the philosophy, but in doing so you must not lose the beauty of the verse in which the poet has set it.

RABBI BEN EZRA

I

" Grow old along with me!
  The best is yet to be,
    The last of life, for which the first was made:
Our times are in His hand
Who saith, 'A whole I planned,
    Youth shows but half; trust God: see all, nor
      be afraid!'

II

Not that, amassing flowers,
Youth sighed, 'Which rose makes ours,
    Which lily leave and then as best recall'?
Not that, admiring stars,
It yearned, 'Nor Jove, nor Mars;
    Mine be some figured flame which blends, tran-
      scends them all'!

THE SPEAKING VOICE

III

Not for such hopes and fears
Annulling youth's brief years,
   Do I remonstrate: folly wide the mark!
Rather I prize the doubt
Low kinds exist without,
    Finished and finite clods, untroubled by a
      spark.

.   .   .   .

VI

Then, welcome each rebuff
That turns earth's smoothness rough,
   Each sting that bids nor sit nor stand but go!
Be our joys three-parts pain!
Strive and hold cheap the strain;
    Learn, nor account the pang; dare, never
      grudge the throe!

VII

For thence—a paradox
Which comforts while it mocks—
   Shall life succeed in that it seems to fail:
What I aspired to be,
And was not, comforts me:
    A brute I might have been, but would not
      sink i' the scale.

.   .   .   .

DIDACTIC POETRY

XXII

Now, who shall arbitrate?
Ten men love what I hate,
　　Shun what I follow, slight what I receive;
Ten, who in ears and eyes
Match me: we all surmise,
　　They, this thing, and I, that: whom shall my
　　　　soul believe?

XXIII

Not on the vulgar mass
Called 'work,' must sentence pass,
　　Things done, that took the eye and had the
　　　　price;
O'er which, from level stand,
The low world laid its hand,
　　Found straightway to its mind, could value in
　　　　a trice:

XXIV

But all, the world's coarse thumb
And finger failed to plumb,
　　So passed in making up the main account:
All instincts immature,
All purposes unsure,
　　That weighed not as his work, yet swelled the
　　　　man's amount:

XXV

Thoughts hardly to be packed
Into a narrow act,
　　Fancies that broke through language and es-
　　　　caped;

THE SPEAKING VOICE

All I could never be,
All, men ignored in me,
  This, I was worth to God, whose wheel the
    pitcher shaped."

  .   .   .   .

—Robert Browning.

FORBEARANCE

" Hast thou named all the birds without a gun?
Loved the wood-rose, and left it on its stalk?
At rich men's tables eaten bread and pulse?
Unarmed, faced danger with a heart of trust?
And loved so well a high behavior,
In man or maid, that thou from speech re-
    frained,
Nobility more nobly to repay?
O, be my friend, and teach me to be thine!"

EACH AND ALL

" Little thinks, in the field, yon red-cloaked clown
Of thee from the hill-top looking down;
The heifer that lows in the upland farm,
Far-heard, lows not thine ear to charm;
The sexton, tolling his bell at noon,
Deems not that great Napoleon
Stops his horse and lists with delight,
Whilst his files sweep round yon Alpine height;
Nor knowest thou what argument
Thy life to thy neighbor's creed has lent.

148

DIDACTIC POETRY

All are needed by each one;
Nothing is fair or good alone.
I thought the sparrow's note from heaven,
Singing at dawn on the alder bough;
I brought him home, in his nest, at even;
He sings the song, but it cheers not now,
For I did not bring home the river and sky;—
He sang to my ear,—they sang to my eye.
The delicate shells lay on the shore;
The bubbles of the latest wave
Fresh pearls to their enamel gave,
And the bellowing of the savage sea
Greeted their safe escape to me.
I wiped away the weeds and foam,
I fetched my sea-born treasures home;
But the poor, unsightly, noisome things
Had left their beauty on the shore
With the sun and the sand and the wild up-
    roar.
The lover watched his graceful maid,
As 'mid the virgin train she strayed,
Nor knew her beauty's best attire
Was woven still by the snow-white choir.
At last she came to his hermitage,
Like the bird from the woodlands to the cage;—
The gay enchantment was undone,
A gentle wife, but fairy none.
Then I said, 'I covet truth;
Beauty is unripe childhood's cheat;
I leave it behind with the games of youth':—
As I spoke, beneath my feet
The ground-pine curled its pretty wreath,
Running over the club-moss burrs;

THE SPEAKING VOICE

I inhaled the violet's breath;
Around me stood the oaks and firs;
Pine-cones and acorns lay on the ground;
Over me soared the eternal sky,
Full of light and of deity;
Again I saw, again I heard,
The rolling river, the morning bird;—
Beauty through my senses stole;
I yielded myself to the perfect whole."

—R. W. EMERSON.

VI

THE SHORT STORY

IN your work on the short story I want
you to study two distinctive types: the
story which depends for its interest on incident and the story which depends for its
interest on character development.

I want you to study side by side with this
story of Mary E. Wilkins one of Rudyard
Kipling's *Jungle Tales*. "Rikki Tikki Tavi"
is a good example of the story of incident. The
"Revolt of 'Mother'" is a good example of
the story of "character development." Both
these tales obey the highest laws of the short
story, and both demand of the reader sustained vigor of the imagination and spirit,
and so of tone and expression. Both stories
are simple in structure and in language.

The interest of Mrs. Freeman's story lies in the characters and depends for its quality of movement upon the increasing vitality of the relation between the characters. Interest in Mr. Kipling's story is one of incident. It is more difficult to catch and hold the attention of an audience with the New England story than with the Jungle tale, because its interest is more subtle and its movement less pronounced. The reader of Mrs. Freeman's story must understand the type of character she has presented and be able to feel and suggest the individual atmosphere of each character. The reader of "Rikki Tikki Tavi" must be obsessed with the brave spirit of the little mongoose, and suggest his atmosphere of courage and unflinching purpose. Mrs. Freeman's story must move in the interpretation with the movement of the characters in relation to one another and in relation to the underlying philosophy of the situation. Mr. Kipling's story moves along a path of progressive dramatic incident to an intense climax.

THE SHORT STORY

THE REVOLT OF "MOTHER"[1]

BY MARY E. WILKINS

"Father!"

"What is it?"

"What are them men diggin' over there in the field for?"

[There was a sudden dropping and enlarging of the lower part of the old man's face, as if some heavy weight had settled therein; he shut his mouth tight, and went on harnessing the great bay mare. He hustled the collar on to her neck with a jerk.][2]

"Father!"

The old man slapped the saddle upon the mare's back.

"Look here, father, I want to know what them men are diggin' over in the field for, an' I'm goin' to know."

"I wish you'd go into the house, mother, an' 'tend to your own affairs," [the old man said then. He ran his words together, and his speech was almost as inarticulate as a growl.

[1] From *A New England Nun and Other Stories*. Copyright, 1891, by Harper & Brothers.

[2] The brackets indicate portions of the text which may be omitted in presenting the story from the platform.

But the woman understood; it was her most native tongue.] "I ain't goin' into the house till you tell me what them men are doin' over there in the field," said she.

[Then she stood waiting. She was a small woman, short and straight-waisted like a child in her brown cotton gown. Her forehead was mild and benevolent between the smooth curves of gray hair; there were meek downward lines about her nose and mouth; but her eyes, fixed upon the old man, looked as if the meekness had been the result of her own will, never of the will of another.]

They were in the barn, standing before the wide-open doors. The spring air, full of the smell of growing grass and unseen blossoms, came in their faces. [The deep yard in front was littered with farm-wagons and piles of wood; on the edges, close to the fence and the house, the grass was a vivid green, and there were some dandelions.]

The old man glanced doggedly at his wife as he tightened the last buckles on the harness. [She looked as immovable to him as one of the rocks in his pasture-land, bound to the earth with generations of blackberry-vines. He slapped the reins over the horse and started forth from the barn.]

"*Father!*" said she.

The old man pulled up. "What is it?"

"I want to know what them men are diggin' over there in that field for."

"They're diggin' a cellar, I s'pose, if you've got to know."

"A cellar for what?"

"A barn."

"A barn? You ain't goin' to build a barn over there where we was goin' to have a house, father?"

The old man said not another word. He hurried the horse into the farm-wagon, and clattered out of the yard, [jouncing as sturdily on his seat as a boy].

The woman stood a moment looking after him, then she went out of the barn across a corner of the yard to the house. The house, standing at right angles with the great barn and a long reach of sheds and out-buildings, was infinitesimal compared with them. It was scarcely as commodious for people as the little boxes under the barn eaves were for the doves.

A pretty girl's face, pink and delicate as a flower, was looking out of one of the house windows. [She was watching three men who were digging over in the field which bounded the yard near the road-line. She turned quietly when the woman entered.]

"What are they digging for, mother?" said she. "Did he tell you?"

"They're diggin' for—a cellar for a new barn."

155

"Oh, mother, he ain't going to build another barn?"

"That's what he says."

A boy stood before the kitchen glass combing his hair. [He combed slowly and painstakingly, arranging his brown hair in a smooth hillock over his forehead. He did not seem to pay any attention to the conversation.]

"Sammy, did you know father was going to build a new barn?" asked the girl.

The boy combed assiduously.

"Sammy!"

[He turned, and showed a face like his father's under his smooth crest of hair.] "Yes, I s'pose I did," he said, reluctantly.

"How long have you known it?" asked his mother.

"'Bout three months, I guess."

"Why didn't you tell of it?"

"Didn't think 'twould do no good."

"I don't see what father wants another barn for," said the girl, in her sweet, slow voice. She turned again to the window and stared out at the digging men in the field. Her tender, sweet face was full of a gentle distress. [Her forehead was as bald and innocent as a baby's, with the light hair strained back from it in a row of curl-papers. She was quite large, but her soft curves did not look as if they covered muscles.]

156

Her mother looked sternly at the boy. "Is he goin' to buy more cows?" said she.

The boy did not reply; he was tying his shoes.

"Sammy, I want you to tell me if he's goin' to buy more cows."

"I s'pose he is."

"How many?"

"Four, I guess."

His mother said nothing more. She went into the pantry, and there was a clatter of dishes. The boy got his cap from a nail behind the door, took an old arithmetic from the shelf, and started for school. [He was lightly built, but clumsy. He went out of the yard with a curious spring in the hips that made his loose home-made jacket tilt up in the rear.]

The girl went to the sink, and began to wash the dishes that were piled up there. Her mother came promptly out of the pantry, and shoved her aside. "You wipe 'em," she said; "I'll wash. There's a good many this mornin'."

The mother plunged her hands vigorously into the water; the girl wiped the plates slowly and dreamily. "Mother," said she, "don't you think it's too bad father's going to build that new barn, much as we need a decent house to live in?"

Her mother scrubbed a dish fiercely. "You 'ain't found out yet we're women-folks, Nanny

Penn," said she. "You 'ain't seen enough of men-folks yet to. One of these days you'll find it out, an' then you'll know that we know only what men-folks think we do, so far as any use of it goes, an' how we'd ought to reckon men-folks in with Providence, an' not complain of what they do any more than we do of the weather."

"I don't care; I don't believe George is anything like that, anyhow," [said Nanny. Her delicate face flushed pink, her lips pouted softly, as if she were going to cry].

"You wait an' see. I guess George Eastman ain't no better than other men. You hadn't ought to judge father, though. He can't help it, 'cause he don't look at things jest the way we do. An' we've been pretty comfortable here, after all. The roof don't leak—'ain't never but once—that's one thing. Father's kept it shingled right up."

"I do wish we had a parlor."

"I guess it won't hurt George Eastman any to come to see you in a nice clean kitchen. I guess a good many girls don't have as good a place as this. Nobody's ever heard me complain."

"I 'ain't complained either, mother."

"Well, I don't think you'd better, a good father an' a good home as you've got. S'pose your father made you go out an' work for your livin'? Lots of girls have to that ain't no stronger an' better able to than you be."

Sarah Penn washed the frying-pan with a conclusive air. She scrubbed the outside of it as faithfully as the inside. She was a masterly keeper of her box of a house. Her one living-room never seemed to have in it any of the dust which the friction of life with inanimate matter produces. [She swept, and there seemed to be no dirt to go before the broom; she cleaned, and one could see no difference. She was like an artist so perfect that he has apparently no art. To-day she got out a mixing-bowl and a board, and rolled some pies, and there was no more flour upon her than upon her daughter who was doing finer work. Nanny was to be married in the fall, and she was sewing on some white cambric and embroidery. She sewed industriously, while her mother cooked; her soft, milk-white hands and wrists showed whiter than her delicate work.]

"We must have the stove moved out in the shed before long," said Mrs. Penn. "Talk about not havin' things, it's been a real blessin' to be able to put a stove up in that shed in hot weather. Father did one good thing when he fixed that stove-pipe out there."

Sarah Penn's face as she rolled her pies had that expression of meek vigor which might have characterized one of the New Testament saints.

159

She was making mince - pies. Her husband, Adoniram Penn, liked them better than any other kind. [She baked twice a week. Adoniram often liked a piece of pie between meals. She hurried this morning. It had been later than usual when she began, and she wanted to have a pie baked for dinner.] However deep a resentment she might be forced to hold against her husband, she would never fail in sedulous attention to his wants.

[Nobility of character manifests itself at loopholes when it is not provided with large doors. Sarah Penn's showed itself to-day in flaky dishes of pastry.] She made the pies faithfully, while across the table she could see, when she glanced up from her work, the sight that rankled in her patient and steadfast soul—the digging of the cellar of the new barn in the place where Adoniram forty years ago had promised her their new house should stand.

The pies were done for dinner. Adoniram and Sammy were home a few minutes after twelve o'clock. [The dinner was eaten with serious haste. There was never much conversation at the table in the Penn family. Adoniram asked a blessing, and they ate promptly, then rose up and went about their work.

Sammy went back to school, taking soft sly lopes out of the yard like a rabbit. He wanted a game of marbles before school, and feared his father would give him some chores to do. Adoniram hastened to the door and called after him, but he was out of sight.

"I don't see what you let him go for, mother," said he. "I wanted him to help me unload that wood."]

Adoniram went to work out in the yard unloading wood from the wagon. Sarah put away the dinner dishes, while Nanny took down her curl-papers and changed her dress. She was going down to the store to buy some more embroidery and thread.

When Nanny was gone, Mrs. Penn went to the door. "Father!" she called.

"Well, what is it!"

"I want to see you jest a minute, father."

"I can't leave this wood, nohow. I've got to git it unloaded an' go for a load of gravel afore two o'clock. Sammy had ought to helped me. You hadn't ought to let him go to school so early."

"I want to see you jest a minute."

"I tell ye I can't, nohow, mother."

"Father, you come here." [Sarah Penn stood in the door like a queen; she held her head as if it bore a crown; there was that patience which makes authority royal in her voice.] Adoniram went.

Mrs. Penn led the way into the kitchen, and pointed to a chair. "Sit down, father," [said she;] "I've got somethin' I want to say to you."

[He sat down heavily; his face was quite stolid, but he looked at her with restive eyes.] "Well, what is it, mother?"

"I want to know what you're buildin' that new barn for, father?"

"I 'ain't got nothin' to say about it."

"It can't be you think you need another barn?"

"I tell ye I 'ain't got nothin' to say about it, mother; an' I ain't goin' to say nothin'."

"Be you goin' to buy more cows?"

Adoniram did not reply; he shut his mouth tight.

"I know you be, as well as I want to. Now, father, look here"—[Sarah Penn had not sat down; she stood before her husband in the humble fashion of a Scripture woman—] "I'm goin' to talk real plain to you; I never have sence I married you, but I'm goin' to now. I 'ain't never complained, an' I ain't goin' to complain now, but I'm goin' to talk plain. You see this room here, father; you look at it well. You see there ain't no carpet on the floor, an' you see the paper is all dirty an' droppin' off the walls. We 'ain't had no new paper on it for ten year, an' then I put it on myself, an' it didn't cost but ninepence a roll. You see this room, father; it's all the one I've had to work in an' eat in an' sit in sence we was married. There ain't another woman in the whole town whose husband 'ain't got half the means you have but what's got better. It's all the room Nanny's got to have her company in; an' there ain't one of her mates but what's got better, an' their fathers not so able as hers is. It's all the room she'll have to be married in. What would you have thought, father, if we had had our weddin' in a room no better than this? I was married in my mother's parlor, with a carpet on the floor, an' stuffed furniture, an' a mahogany card-table. An' this is all the room my daughter will have to be married in. Look here, father!"

Sarah Penn went across the room as though it were a tragic stage. She flung open a door and disclosed a tiny bedroom, only large enough for a bed and bureau, with a path between. "There, father," said she—"there's all the room I've had to sleep in forty year. All my children were born there—the two that died, an' the two that's livin'. I was sick with a fever there."

She stepped to another door and opened it. [It led into the small, ill-lighted pantry.] "Here," [said she,] "is all the buttery I've got—every place I've got for my dishes, to set away my victuals in, an' to keep my milk-pans in. Father, I've been takin' care of the milk of six cows in this place, an' now you're goin' to build a new barn, an' keep more cows, an' give me more to do in it."

She threw open another door. A narrow crooked flight of stairs wound upward from it. "There, father," said she, "I want you to look at the stairs that go up to them two unfinished chambers that are all the places our son an' daughter have had to sleep in all their lives. There ain't a prettier girl in town nor a more ladylike one than Nanny, an' that's the place she has to sleep in. It ain't so good as your horse's stall; it ain't so warm an' tight."

Sarah Penn went back and stood before her husband. "Now, father," said she, "I want to know if you think you're doin' right an' accordin' to what you profess. Here, when we was married, forty year ago, you promised me faithful that we should have a new house built in that lot over in the field before the year was out. You said you had money enough, an' you wouldn't ask me to live in no such place as this. It is forty year now, an' you've been makin' more money, an' I've been savin' of it for you ever since, an' you 'ain't built no house yet. You've built sheds an' cow-houses an' one new barn, an' now you're goin' to build another. Father, I want to know if you think it's right. You're lodgin' your dumb beasts better than you are your own flesh an' blood. I want to know if you think it's right."

"I 'ain't got nothin' to say."

"You can't say nothin' without ownin' it ain't right, father. An' there's another thing —I 'ain't complained; I've got along forty year, an' I s'pose I should forty more, if it wa'n't for that—if we don't have another house, Nanny she can't live with us after she's married. She'll have to go somewheres else to live away from us, an' it don't seem as if I could have it so, noways, father. She wa'n't ever strong. She's got considerable color, but there wa'n't never any backbone to her. I've always took the heft of everything off her, an' she ain't fit to keep house an' do everything herself. She'll be all worn out inside a year. Think of her doin' all the washin' an' ironin' an' bakin' with them soft white hands an' arms, an' sweepin'! I can't have it so, noways, father."

[Mrs. Penn's face was burning; her mild eyes gleamed. She had pleaded her little cause like a Webster; she had ranged from severity to pathos; but her opponent employed that obstinate silence which makes eloquence futile with mocking echoes. Adoniram arose clumsily.]

"Father, 'ain't you got nothin' to say?" said Mrs. Penn.

"I've got to go off after that load of gravel. I can't stan' here talkin' all day."

"Father, won't you think it over, an' have a house built there instead of a barn?"

"I 'ain't got nothin' to say."

Adoniram shuffled out. Mrs. Penn went into her bedroom. When she came out her eyes were red. [She had a roll of unbleached cotton cloth. She spread it out on the kitchen table, and began cutting out some shirts for her husband. The men over in the field had a team to help them this afternoon; she could hear their halloos. She had a scanty pattern for the shirts; she had to plan and piece the sleeves.]

Nanny came home with her embroidery, and sat down with her needlework. [She had taken down her curl-papers, and there was a soft roll of fair hair like an aureole over her forehead;] her face was as delicately fine and clear as porcelain. Suddenly she looked up, and the tender red flamed all over her face and neck. "Mother," [said she].

"What say?"

"I've been thinking—I don't see how we're goin' to have any—wedding in this room. I'd be ashamed to have his folks come if we didn't have anybody else."

"Mebbe we can have some new paper before then; I can put it on. I guess you won't have no call to be ashamed of your belongin's."

"We might have the wedding in the new barn," [said Nanny, with gentle pettishness]. "Why, mother, what makes you look so?"

Mrs. Penn had started, and was staring at

166 .

her with a curious expression. [She turned again to her work and spread out a pattern carefully on the cloth.] "Nothin'," said she.

[Presently Adoniram clattered out of the yard in his two-wheeled dump-cart, standing as proudly upright as a Roman charioteer. Mrs. Penn opened the door and stood there a minute looking out; the halloos of the men sounded louder.

It seemed to her all through the spring months that she heard nothing but the halloos and the noises of saws and hammers. The new barn grew fast. It was a fine edifice for this little village. Men came on pleasant Sundays, in their meeting suits and clean shirtbosoms, and stood around it admiringly. Mrs. Penn did not speak of it, and Adoniram did not mention it to her, although sometimes, upon a return from inspecting it, he bore himself with injured dignity.

"It's a strange thing how your mother feels about the new barn," he said, confidentially, to Sammy one day.

Sammy only grunted after an odd fashion for a boy; he had learned it from his father.]

The barn was all completed ready for use by the third week in July. Adoniram had planned to move his stock in on Wednesday; on Tuesday he received a letter which changed his plans. He came in with it early in the morning. "Sammy's been to the post-office," said he, "an' I've got a letter from Hiram." Hiram was Mrs. Penn's brother, who lived in Vermont.

["Well," said Mrs. Penn, "what does he say about the folks?"

"I guess they're all right.] He says he thinks if I come up-country right off there's a chance to buy jest the kind of a horse I want." [He stared reflectively out of the window at the new barn.

Mrs. Penn was making pies. She went on clapping the rolling-pin into the crust, although she was very pale, and her heart beat loudly.]

"I dun know but what I'd better go," [said Adoniram]. "I hate to go off jest now, right in the midst of hayin', but the ten-acre lot's cut, an' I guess Rufus an' the others can git along without me three or four days. I can't get a horse round here to suit me, nohow, an' I've got to have another for all that wood-haulin' in the fall. I told Hiram to watch out, an' if he got wind of a good horse to let me know. I guess I'd better go."

"I'll get out your clean shirt an' collar," [said Mrs. Penn, calmly].

She laid out Adoniram's Sunday suit and his clean clothes on the bed in the little bedroom. She got his shaving-water and razor ready. At last she buttoned on his collar and fastened his black cravat.

Adoniram never wore his collar and cravat

except on extra occasions. He held his head high, with a rasped dignity. [When he was all ready, with his coat and hat brushed, and a lunch of pie and cheese in a paper bag, he hesitated on the threshold of the door. He looked at his wife, and his manner was defiantly apologetic.] "*If* them cows come to-day, Sammy can drive 'em into the new barn," [said he]; "an' when they bring the hay up, they can pitch it in there."

["Well," replied Mrs. Penn.

Adoniram set his shaven face ahead and started. When he had cleared the door-step, he turned and looked back with a kind of nervous solemnity.] "I shall be back by Saturday if nothin' happens," [said he].

"Do be careful, father," returned his wife.

She stood in the door with Nanny at her elbow and watched him out of sight. Her eyes had a strange, doubtful expression in them; her peaceful forehead was contracted. She went in, and about her baking again. Nanny sat sewing. Her wedding-day was drawing nearer, and she was getting pale and thin with her steady sewing. Her mother kept glancing at her.

"Have you got that pain in your side this mornin'?" [she asked.]

"A little."

Mrs. Penn's face, as she worked, changed,

169

her perplexed forehead smoothed, her eyes were steady, her lips firmly set. [She formed a maxim for herself, although incoherently with her un-lettered thoughts. "Unsolicited opportunities are the guide-posts of the Lord to the new roads of life," she repeated in effect, and she made up her mind to her course of action.]

"S'posin' I *had* wrote to Hiram," she muttered once when she was in the pantry. "S'posin' I had wrote an' asked him if he knew of any horse? But I didn't, an' father's goin' wa'n't none of my doin'. It looks like a providence." Her voice rang out quite loud at the last.

"What you talkin' about, mother?" [called Nanny.]

"Nothin'."

Mrs. Penn hurried her baking at eleven o'clock it was all done. The load of hay from the west field came slowly down the cart track, and drew up at the new barn. Mrs. Penn ran out. "Stop!" she screamed—"stop!"

[The men stopped and looked; Sammy up-reared from the top of the load, and stared at his mother].

"Stop!" she cried out again.] "Don't you put the hay in that barn; put it in the old one."

"Why, he said to put it in here," returned one of the haymakers, wonderingly. [He was a young man, a neighbor's son, whom Adoniram hired by the year to help on the farm.]

"Don't you put the hay in the new barn; there's room enough in the old one, ain't there?" [said Mrs. Penn.]

"Room enough," [returned the hired man, in his thick, rustic tones]. "Didn't need the new barn, nohow, far as room's concerned. Well, I s'pose he changed his mind." He took hold of the horses' bridles.

[Mrs. Penn went back to the house. Soon the kitchen windows were darkened, and a fragrance like warm honey came into the room.]

Nanny laid down her work. "I thought father wanted them to put the hay into the new barn?" [she said, wonderingly.]

"It's all right," replied her mother.

[Sammy slid down from the load of hay, and came in to see if dinner was ready.

"I ain't goin' to get a regular dinner to-day, as long as father's gone," said his mother. "I've let the fire go out. You can have some bread an' milk an' pie. I thought we could get along." She set out some bowls of milk, some bread, and a pie on the kitchen table. "You'd better eat your dinner now," said she. "You might jest as well get through with it. I want you to help me afterward."]

Nanny and Sammy stared at each other. There was something strange in their mother's manner. Mrs. Penn [did not eat anything herself. She] went into the pantry, and they heard her moving dishes while they ate. Presently she came out with a pile of plates. She got the clothes-basket out of the shed, and packed them in it. Nanny and Sammy watched. She brought out cups and saucers, and put them in with the plates.

"What you goin' to do, mother?" inquired Nanny, in a timid voice. [A sense of something unusual made her tremble, as if it were a ghost. Sammy rolled his eyes over his pie.]

"You'll see what I'm goin' to do," [replied Mrs. Penn]. "If you're through, Nanny, I want you to go up-stairs an' pack up your things; an' I want you, Sammy, to help me take down the bed in the bedroom."

"Oh, mother, what for?" gasped Nanny.

"You'll see."

During the next few hours a feat·was performed by this simple, pious New England mother which was equal in its way to Wolfe's storming of the Heights of Abraham. It took no more genius and audacity of bravery for Wolfe to cheer his wondering soldiers up those steep precipices, under the sleeping eyes of the enemy, than for Sarah Penn, at the head of her children, to move all their little household goods into the new barn while her husband was away.

[Nanny and Sammy followed their mother's instructions without a murmur; indeed, they

172

were overawed. There is a certain uncanny
and superhuman quality about all such purely
original undertakings as their mother's was to
them. Nanny went back and forth with her
light loads, and Sammy tugged with sober
energy.]

At five o'clock in the afternoon the little
house in which the Penns had lived for forty
years had emptied itself into the new barn.

Every builder builds somewhat for unknown
purposes, and is in a measure a prophet. The
architect of Adoniram Penn's barn, while he
designed it for the comfort of four-footed animals, had planned better than he knew for
the comfort of humans. Sarah Penn saw at a
glance its possibilities. Those great box-stalls,
with quilts hung before them, would make better
bedrooms than the one she had occupied for
forty years, and there was a tight carriage-room.
The harness-room, with its chimney and shelves,
would make a kitchen of her dreams. The
great middle space would make a parlor, by-
and-by, fit for a palace. Up-stairs there was
as much room as down. With partitions and
windows, what a house would there be! Sarah
looked at the row of stanchions before the allotted space for cows, and reflected that she
would have her front entry there.

At six o'clock the stove was up in the harness-
room, the kettle was boiling, and the table set

for tea. It looked almost as homelike as the abandoned house across the yard ever had done. The young hired man milked, and Sarah directed him calmly to bring the milk to the new barn. He came gaping, dropping little blots of foam from the brimming pails on the grass. Before the next morning he had spread the story of Adoniram Penn's wife moving into the new barn all over the little village. [Men assembled in the store and talked it over, women with shawls over their heads scuttled into one another's houses before their work was done. Any deviation from the ordinary course of life in this quiet town was enough to stop all progress in it. Everybody paused to look at the staid, independent figure on the side track. There was a difference of opinion with regard to her. Some held her to be insane; some, of a lawless and rebellious spirit.]

Friday the minister went to see her. It was in the forenoon, and she was at the barn door shelling pease for dinner. She looked up and returned his salutation with dignity, then she went on with her work. [She did not invite him in. The saintly expression of her face remained fixed, but there was an angry flush over it.]

The minister stood awkwardly before her and talked. [She handled the pease as if they were bullets. At last she looked up, and her eyes

174

showed the spirit that her meek front had covered for a lifetime.]

"There ain't no use talkin', Mr. Hersey," said she. "I've thought it all over an' over, an' I believe I'm doin' what's right. I've made it the subject of prayer, an' it's betwixt me an' the Lord an' Adoniram. There ain't no call for nobody else to worry about it."

"Well, of course, if you have brought it to the Lord in prayer, and feel satisfied that you are doing right, Mrs. Penn," [said the minister, helplessly. His thin, gray-bearded face was pathetic. He was a sickly man; his youthful confidence had cooled; he had to scourge himself up to some of his pastoral duties as relentlessly as a Catholic ascetic, and then he was prostrated by the smart].

"I think it's right jest as much as I think it was right for our forefathers to come over from the old country 'cause they didn't have what belonged to 'em," [said Mrs. Penn]. She arose. [The barn threshold might have been Plymouth Rock from her bearing.] "I don't doubt you mean well, Mr. Hersey," said she, "but there are things people hadn't ought to interfere with. I've been a member of the church for over forty year. I've got my own mind an' my own feet, an' I'm goin' to think my own thoughts an' go my own ways, an' nobody but the Lord is goin' to dictate to me unless I've a mind to

have him. Won't you come in an' set down?
How is Mis' Hersey?"

"She is well, I thank you," [replied the minister. He added some more perplexed apologetic remarks; then he retreated].

He could expound the intricacies of every
character study in the Scriptures, he was com-
petent to grasp the Pilgrim Fathers and all
historical innovators, but Sarah Penn was beyond him. [He could deal with primal cases,
but parallel ones worsted him. But, after all,
although it was aside from his province, he
wondered more how Adoniram Penn would
deal with his wife than how the Lord would.
Everybody shared the wonder. When Adoniram's four new cows arrived, Sarah ordered
three to be put in the old barn, the other in the
house-shed where the cooking-stove had stood.
That added to the excitement. It was whis-
pered that all four cows were domiciled in the
house.]

Toward sunset on Saturday, when Adoniram
was expected home, there was a knot of men
in the road near the new barn. The hired man
had milked, but he still hung around the prem-
ises. Sarah Penn had supper all ready. There
were brown - bread, and baked beans and a
custard pie; it was the supper that Adoniram
loved on a Saturday night. She had on a clean
calico, and she bore herself imperturbably.

Nanny and Sammy kept close at her heels. [Their eyes were large, and Nanny was full of nervous tremors. Still there was to them more pleasant excitement than anything else. An inborn confidence in their mother over their father asserted itself.]

Sammy looked out of the harness-room window. "There he is," he announced, in an awed whisper. [He and Nanny peeped around the casing. Mrs. Penn kept on about her work.] The children watched Adoniram leave the new horse standing in the drive while he went to the house door. It was fastened. Then he went around to the shed. That door was seldom locked, even when the family was away. [The thought how her father would be confronted by the cow flashed upon Nanny. There was a hysterical sob in her throat.] Adoniram emerged from the shed and stood looking about in a dazed fashion. [His lips moved; he was saying something, but they could not hear what it was. The hired man was peeping around a corner of the old barn, but nobody saw him.]

Adoniram took the new horse by the bridle and led him across the yard to the new barn. [Nanny and Sammy slunk close to their mother. The barn doors rolled back, and there stood Adoniram, with the long mild face of the great Canadian farm-horse looking over his shoulder.]

Nanny kept behind her mother, but Sammy

stepped suddenly forward, and stood in front of her.

Adoniram stared at the group. "What on airth you all down here for?" said he. "What's the matter over to the house?"

"We've come here to live, father," said Sammy. His shrill voice quavered out bravely.

"What" [—Adoniram sniffed]—"what is it smells like cookin'?" [said he.] He stepped forward and looked in the open door of the harness-room. Then he turned to his wife. His old bristling face was pale and frightened. "What on airth does this mean, mother?" [he gasped].

"You come in here, father," [said Sarah. She led the way into the harness - room and shut the door]. "Now, father," [said she] "you needn't be scared. I ain't crazy. There ain't nothin' to be upset over. But we've come here to live, an' we're goin' to live here. We've got jest as good a right here as new horses an' cows. The house wa'n't fit for us to live in any longer, an' I made up my mind I wa'n't goin' to stay there. I've done my duty by you forty year, an' I'm goin' to do it now; but I'm goin' to live here. You've got to put in some windows and partitions; an' you'll have to buy some furniture."

"Why, mother!" [the old man gasped.]

"You'd better take your coat off an' get washed—there's the wash-basin—an' then we'll have supper."

178

"Why, mother!"

[Sammy went past the window, leading the new horse to the old barn. The old man saw him and shook his head speechlessly.] He tried to take off his coat, but his arms seemed to lack the power. His wife helped him. She poured some water into the tin basin, and put in a piece of soap. She got the comb and brush, and smoothed his thin gray hair after he had washed. Then she put the beans, hot bread, and tea on the table. Sammy came in, and the family drew up. Adoniram sat looking dazedly at his plate and they waited.

"Ain't you goin' to ask a blessin', father?" [said Sarah.]

And the old man bent his head and mumbled.

All through the meal he stopped eating at intervals, and stared furtively at his wife; but he ate well. The home food tasted good to him, and his old frame was too sturdily healthy to be affected by his mind. But after supper he went out, and sat down on the step of the smaller door at the right of the barn, through which he had meant his Jerseys to pass in stately file, but which Sarah designed for her front house-door, and he leaned his head on his hands.

After the supper dishes were cleared away and the milk-pans washed, Sarah went out to him. The twilight was deepening. There was a clear green glow in the sky. Before them

179

stretched the smooth level of field; in the distance was a cluster of hay-stacks like the huts of a village; the air was very cool and calm and sweet. The landscape might have been an ideal one of peace.

Sarah bent over and touched her husband on one of his thin, sinewy shoulders. "Father!"

The old man's shoulders heaved: he was weeping.

"Why, don't do so, father," said Sarah.

"I'll — put up the — partitions, an' — everything you—want, mother."

Sarah put her apron up to her face; she was overcome by her own triumph.

Adoniram was like a fortress whose walls had no active resistance, and went down the instant the right besieging tools were used. "Why, mother," [he said, hoarsely] "I hadn't no idee you was so set on't as all this comes to."

VII

EPIC POETRY

THE epic poem makes the appeal and demand of essay, lyric poem, and short story in one. If you obey all the laws you have discovered in the study of these first three forms, and use all the power you have developed, you will be able to read effectively this cutting of "Gareth and Lynette." This arrangement was made and presented by Mrs. Mary Everts Ewing, formerly teacher of expression in the University of Iowa. Mrs. Ewing's method in cutting a story, poem, or play is simple and very effective, as her results show. She says, " First study your poem, play, or story as a whole. Consider it from every standpoint: its author, its type, its motive, its philosophy, its structure — in fact, know it. Second: Determine

181

your motive in presenting the poem, play, or story. Third: Define your motive; what phase of the theme do you want to show; what aspect of the story do you want to present; which thread of the plot do you wish to follow. Fourth: Cut everything which does not preserve the theme, phase, or thread you have chosen to present. Fifth: If your condensation now fails to come within the time allotted for its presentation, cut everything you can without sacrificing your theme. Sixth: If you find you have cut more than is necessary, restore that which seems most illuminating to your theme.

Because the arrangement of this one of the "Idylls of the King" has been made for you, do not fail to heed the first rule for preparing such a poem for presentation. Study the complete poem. Do more. Study all the "Idylls of the King." Saturate yourself in the atmosphere of this great epic. Read all the fragmentary poems which foreshadow this masterpiece of Tennyson's. Make your own cutting of "Gareth and Lynette," and

compare it with this one. Study Tennyson's
dedication of this epic.

GARETH AND LYNETTE

" The last tall son of Lot and Bellicent,
And tallest, Gareth, in a showerful spring
Stared at the spate. A slender-shafted Pine
Lost footing, fell, and so was whirl'd away.
'How he went down,' said Gareth, 'as a false knight
Or evil king before my lance if lance
Were mine to use—O senseless cataract,
Bearing all down in thy precipitancy—
And yet thou art but swollen with cold snows,
And mine is living blood: thou dost His will,
The Maker's, and not knowest, and I that know
Have strength and wit, in my good mother's hall
Linger with vacillating obedience,
Prison'd, and kept and coax'd and whistled to—
Since the good mother holds me still a child—

.   .   .   .   .   .

Heaven yield her for it, but in me put force
To weary her ears with one continuous prayer,
Until she let me fly discaged to sweep
Down upon all things base, and dash them dead,
A knight of Arthur, working out his will.'

.   .   .   .   .   .

And Gareth went, and hovering round her chair
Ask'd, ' Mother, tho' ye count me still the child,

.   .   .   .

Man am I grown, a man's work must I do.
Follow the deer? follow the Christ, the King,

THE SPEAKING VOICE

Live pure, speak true, right wrong, follow the
   King—'
  .   .   .   .   .   .

To whom the mother said, ' Yet—wilt thou leave
Thine easeful biding here, and risk thine all,
Life, limbs, for one that is not proven King?
Stay, till the cloud that settles round his birth
Hath lifted but a little. Stay, sweet son.'

And Gareth answer'd quickly, 'Not an hour,
So that ye yield me—I will walk thro' fire,
Mother, to gain it—your full leave to go.'
' Who walks thro' fire will hardly heed the smoke.
Ay, go then, an ye must: only one proof,
Before thou ask the King to make thee knight,
Of thine obedience and thy love to me,
Thy mother,—I demand.'

                           And Gareth cried,
'A hard one, or a hundred, so I go.
Nay—quick! the proof to prove me to the quick!'

But slowly spake the mother looking at him,
'Prince, thou shalt go disguised to Arthur's hall,
And hire thyself to serve for meats and drinks;
Nor shalt thou tell thy name to any one.
And thou shalt serve a twelvemonth and a day.'

Silent awhile was Gareth, then replied,
'The thrall in person may be free in soul,
And I shall see the jousts. Thy son am I,
And since thou art my mother, must obey.
I therefore yield me freely to thy will;'

184

So Gareth all for glory underwent
The sooty yoke of kitchen vassalage;
Ate with young lads his portion by the door,
And couch'd at night with grimy kitchen-knaves.
And Lancelot ever spake him pleasantly,
But Kay, the seneschal, who loved him not,
Would hustle and harry him, and labor him
Beyond his comrade of the hearth, and set
To turn the broach, draw water, or hew wood,
Or grosser tasks; and Gareth bow'd himself
With all obedience to the King, and wrought
All kind of service with a noble ease
That graced the lowliest act in doing it.

So for a month he wrought among the thralls;
But in the weeks that follow'd, the good Queen,
Repentant of the word she made him swear,
And saddening in her childless castle, sent
Arms for her son, and loosed him from his vow.
Shame never made girl redder than Gareth joy.
He laugh'd; he sprang. Whereon he sought
The King alone, and found, and told him all.
' Make me thy knight—in secret! let my name
Be hidd'n, and give me the first quest, I spring
Like flame from ashes.'

          And the King—
'Make thee my knight in secret? yea, but he,
Our noblest brother, and our truest man,
And one with me in all, he needs must know.'

' Let Lancelot know, my King, let Lancelot know,
Thy noblest and thy truest!'

THE SPEAKING VOICE

So with a kindly hand on Gareth's arm
Smiled the great King, and half-unwillingly,
Loving his lusty youthhood, yielded to him.
Then, after summoning Lancelot privily,
'I have given him the first quest: he is not proven.
Look therefore when he calls for this in hall,
Thou get to horse and follow him far away.
Cover the lions on thy shield, and see,
Far as thou mayest, he be nor ta'en nor slain.'

Then that same day there past into the hall
A damsel of high lineage, and cried,
'O King, for thou hast driven the foe without,
See to the foe within! Why sit ye there?
Rest would I not, Sir King, an I were king,
Till ev'n the lonest hold were all as free
From cursed bloodshed, as thine altar-cloth.''

'Comfort thyself,' said Arthur, 'I nor mine
Rest: so my knighthood keep the vows they swore.
The wastest moorland of our realm shall be
Safe, damsel, as the centre of this hall.
What is thy name? thy need?'

'Lynette my name; noble; my need, a knight
To combat for my sister, Lyonors,
A lady of high lineage, of great lands,
And comely, yea, and comelier than myself.
She lives in Castle Perilous: a river
Runs in three loops about her living-place;
And o'er it are three passings, and three knights
Defend the passings, brethren, and a fourth,
And of that four the mightiest, holds her stay'd

In her own castle, and so besieges her
To break her will, and make her wed with him:
. . . . And three of these
Proud in their fantasy call themselves the Day:
Morning-Star, and Noon-Sun, and Evening-Star.
The fourth, who alway rideth arm'd in black,
A huge man-beast of boundless savagery,
He names himself the Night and oftener Death.
And therefore am I come for Lancelot.'

Hereat Sir Gareth call'd from where he rose,'
A head with kindling eyes above the throng,
'A boon, Sir King—this quest!'
. . . . . . And Arthur glancing at him,
Brought down a momentary brow. 'Rough, sud-
den,
And pardonable, worthy to be knight—
Go therefore,' and all hearers were amazed.

But on the damsel's forehead shame, pride,
wrath,
Slew the May-white: she lifted either arm,
'Fie on thee, King! I ask'd for thy chief knight,
And thou hast given me but a kitchen-knave.'
Then ere a man in hall could stay her, turn'd,
Fled down the lane of access to the King,
Took horse, descended the slope street, and past
The weird white gate, and paused without, beside
The field of tourney, murmuring 'kitchen-knave.'

Whereat Sir Gareth donn'd the helm, and took
the shield
And mounted horse and graspt a spear, of grain

Storm-strengthen'd on a windy site, and tipt
With trenchant steel, around him slowly prest
The people, and from out of kitchen came
The thralls in throng, and seeing who had work'd
Lustier than any, and whom they could but love,
Mounted in arms, threw up their caps and cried,
'God bless the King, and all his fellowship!'
And on thro' lanes of shouting Gareth rode
Down the slope street, and past without the gate.

But by the field of tourney lingering yet
Mutter'd the damsel, 'Wherefore did the King
Scorn me?—O sweet heaven!   O fie upon him—
His kitchen-knave.'

              To whom Sir Gareth drew
Shining in arms, 'Damsel, the quest is mine.
Lead, and I follow.'   She thereat, 'Hence!
Avoid, thou smellest all of kitchen-grease.
And look who comes behind,' for there was Kay.
'Knowest thou not me? thy master?   I am Kay.
We lack thee by the hearth.'

              And Gareth to him,
'Master no more! too well I know thee, ay—
The most ungentle knight in Arthur's hall.'
'Have at thee then,' said Kay: they shock'd, and
    Kay
Fell shoulder-slipt, and Gareth cried again,
'Lead, and I follow,' and fast away she fled.

So till the dusk that follow'd evensong
Rode on the two, reviler and reviled;

Then after one long slope was mounted, saw,
A gloomy-gladed hollow; and shouts
Ascended, and there brake a servingman
Flying from out of the black wood, and crying,
'They have bound my lord to cast him in the
    mere.'
Then Gareth, 'Bound am I to right the wrong'd,
But straitlier bound am I to bide with thee.'
And when the damsel spake contemptuously,
'Lead and I follow,' Gareth cried again,
'Follow, I lead!' so down among the pines
He plunged; and there, blackshadow'd nigh the
    mere,
Saw six tall men haling a seventh along,
A stone about his neck to drown him in it.
Three with good blows he quieted, but three
Fled thro' the pines; and Gareth loosed the stone
From off his neck, then in the mere beside
Tumbled it; oilily bubbled up the mere.
Last, Gareth loosed his bonds and on free feet
Set him, a stalwart Baron, Arthur's friend.

    So when, next morn, the lord whose life he saved
Had, some brief space, convey'd them on their
      way
And left them with God-speed, Sir Gareth spake,
'Lead and I follow.'   Haughtily she replied,

    ' I fly no more: I allow thee for an hour.
For hard by here is one will overthrow
And slay thee; then will I to court again,
And shame the King for only yielding me
My champion from the ashes of his hearth.'

To whom Sir Gareth answer'd courteously,
'Say thou thy say, and I will do my deed.

Then to the shore of one of those long loops
Wherethro' the serpent river coil'd, they came.
And therebefore the lawless warrior paced
Unarm'd, and calling, 'Damsel, is this he,
The champion ye have brought from Arthur's
    hall,
For whom we let thee pass?' 'Nay, nay,' she said,
'Sir Morning-Star. The King in utter scorn
Of thee and thy much folly hath sent thee here
His kitchen-knave: and look thou to thyself:
See that he fall not on thee suddenly,
And slay thee unarm'd: he is not knight but
    knave.'
And Gareth silent gazed upon the knight,
Who stood a moment, ere his horse was brought.

Then she that watch'd him, 'Wherefore stare
    ye so?
Thou shakest in thy fear: there yet is time:
Flee down the valley before he get to horse.
Who will cry shame? Thou art not knight but
    knave.'

Said Gareth, 'Damsel, whether knave or knight,
Far liefer had I fight a score of times
Than hear thee so missay me and revile.
Fair words were best for him who fights for thee;
But truly foul are better, for they send
That strength of anger thro' mine arms, I know
That I shall overthrow him.'

And he that bore
The star, being mounted, cried from o'er the
    bridge,
'A kitchen-knave, and sent in scorn of me!
Such fight not I, but answer scorn with scorn.
Avoid: for it beseemeth not a knave
To ride with such a lady.'

                    'Dog, thou liest.
I spring from loftier lineage than thine own.'
He spake; and all at fiery speed the two
Shock'd on the central bridge.
. . . . . . And either knight at once
Fell, as if dead; but quickly rose and drew,
And Gareth lash'd so fiercely with his brand
He drave his enemy backward down the bridge,
The damsel crying, 'Well-stricken kitchen-knave!'
Till Gareth's shield was cloven; but one stroke
Laid him that clove it grovelling on the ground.

Then cried the fall'n, 'Take not my life: I
    yield.'
And Gareth, 'So this damsel ask it of me
Good—I accord it easily as a grace.
    .   .   .   .   .   .
Thy life is thine at her command. Arise
And quickly pass to Arthur's hall, and say
His kitchen-knave hath sent thee. See thou
    crave
His pardon for thy breaking of his laws.
Myself, when I return, will plead for thee.
Thy shield is mine—farewell; and, damsel, thou,
Lead, and I follow.'

And fast away she fled.
Then when he came upon her, spake, 'Methought,
Knave, when I watch'd thee striking on the bridge
The savor of thy kitchen came upon me
A little faintlier: but the wind hath changed:
I scent it twentyfold.' And then she sang,
"O morning-star that smilest in the blue,
O star, my morning dream hath proven true,
Smile sweetly, thou! my love hath smiled on me."

'But thou begone, take counsel, and away,
For hard by here is one that guards a ford—
The second brother in their fool's parable—
Will pay thee all thy wages, and to boot.
Care not for shame: thou art not knight but knave.'
To whom Sir Gareth answer'd, laughingly,
'The knave that doth thee service as full knight
Is all as good, meseems, as any knight
Toward thy sister's freeing.'

'Ay, Sir Knave!
Ay, ay,' she said, 'but thou shalt meet thy match.'

So when they touch'd the second river-loop,
Huge on a huge red horse, and all in mail
Burnish'd to blinding, shown the Noonday Sun,
Whom Gareth met midstream: no room was there
For lance or tourney-skill: four strokes they struck
With sword, and these were mighty; the new knight
Had fear he might be shamed; but as the Sun
Heaved up a ponderous arm to strike the fifth,
The hoof of his horse slipt in the stream, the stream
Descended, and the Sun was wash'd away.

Then Gareth laid his lance athwart the ford;
So drew him home; but he that fought no more,
As being all bone-batter'd on the rock,
Yielded; and Gareth sent him to the King.
'Myself when I return will plead for thee.
Lead, and I follow.' Quietly she led.
'Hath not the good wind, damsel, changed again?'
'Nay, not a point: nor art thou victor here.
There lies a ridge of slate across the ford;
His horse thereon stumbled—and once again she
    sang:

  '"O birds, that warble to the morning sky,
O birds that warble as the day goes by,
Sing sweetly; twice my love hath smiled on me."

   .   .   .   .

  'There stands the third fool of their allegory.'
For there beyond a bridge of treble bow,
The knight that named him Star of Evening stood.

  And Gareth, 'Wherefore waits the madman
    there
Naked in open dayshine?' 'Nay,' she cried,
'Not naked, only wrapt in harden'd skins.'

            Then that other blew
A hard and deadly note upon the horn.
'Approach and arm me!' . . . .
. . . . And forthwith
They madly hurl'd together on the bridge;
And Gareth overthrew him, lighted, drew,

  .   .   .   .

But up like fire he started: and as oft
As Gareth brought him grovelling on his knees,
So many a time he vaulted up again;
Till Gareth panted hard, and his great heart,
Foredooming all his trouble was in vain,
Labor'd within him, for he seem'd as one
That all in later, sadder age begins
To war against ill uses of a life,
But these from all his life arise, and cry,
'Thou hast made us lords, and canst not put us
    down!'
He half despairs; so Gareth seem'd to strike
Vainly, the damsel clamoring all the while,
'Well done, knave - knight, well - stricken, O good
    knight-knave—
Shame me not, shame me not. I have prophe-
    sied—
Strike, thou art worthy of the Table Round—
His arms are old, he trusts the harden'd skin—
Strike—strike—the wind will never change again.'

   And Gareth hearing ever stronglier smote
And hew'd great pieces of his armor off him,
But lash'd in vain against the harden'd skin,
And could not wholly bring him under, more
Than loud Southwesterns, rolling ridge on ridge,
The buoy that rides at sea, and dips and springs
Forever; till at length Sir Gareth's brand
Clash'd his, and brake it utterly to the hilt.
'I have thee now'; but forth that other sprang,
And, all unknightlike, writhed his wiry arms
Around him, till he felt, despite his mail,
Strangled, but straining ev'n his uttermost

Cast, and so hurl'd him headlong o'er the bridge
Down to the river, sink or swim, and cried,
'Lead, and I follow.'

                      But the damsel said,
'I lead no longer; ride thou at my side;
Thou art the kingliest of all kitchen-knaves.

   '"O trefoil, sparkling on the rainy plain,
O rainbow with three colors after rain,
Shine sweetly: thrice my love hath smiled on me."

   'Sir — and, good faith, I fain had added —
      Knight,
But that I heard thee call thyself a knave,—
Shamed am I that I so rebuked, reviled,
Missaid thee; noble I am; and thought the King
Scorn'd me and mine; and now thy pardon, friend.'

   .   .   .   .

   'Damsel,' he said, 'ye be not all to blame,
Saving that ye mistrusted our good King
Would handle scorn, or yield thee, asking, one
Not fit to cope thy quest.   .   .   .   .
   .   .   .   .   .   . Good sooth! I hold
He scarce is knight who lets
His heart be stirr'd with any foolish heat
At any gentle damsel's waywardness.
Shamed? care not! thy foul sayings fought for me:
And seeing now thy words are fair, methinks,
There rides no knight, not Lancelot, his great self,
Hath force to quell me.' . , ...
   .   .   .   .   .   . 'Look,
Who comes behind?'

THE SPEAKING VOICE

          For one—delay'd at first
Thro' helping back the dislocated Kay
Sir Lancelot, having swum the river-loops—
His blue shield-lions cover'd—softly drew
Behind the twain, and when he saw the star
Gleam, on Sir Gareth's turning to him, cried,
'Stay, felon knight, I avenge me for my friend.'

    And Gareth crying prick'd against the cry;
But when they closed—in a moment—at one touch
Of that skill'd spear, the wonder of the world—
Went sliding down so easily, and fell,
That when he found the grass within his hands
He laugh'd; the laughter jarr'd upon Lynette:
Harshly she ask'd him, 'Shamed and overthrown,
And tumbled back into the kitchen-knave,
Why laugh ye? that ye blew your boast in vain?'
'Nay, noble damsel, but that I, the son
Of old King Lot and good Queen Bellicent,
And victor of the bridges and the ford,
And knight of Arthur, here lie thrown by whom
I know not, all thro' mere unhappiness—
Device and sorcery and unhappiness—
Out, sword; we are thrown!' And Lancelot an-
    swer'd, 'Prince,
O Gareth—thro' the mere unhappiness
Of one who came to help thee, not to harm,
Lancelot, and all as glad to find thee whole,
As on the day when Arthur knighted him.

  ·   ·   ·   ·   ·   ·   ·

          'O damsel, be ye wise
To call him shamed, who is but overthrown?
Thrown have I been, nor once, but many a time.

Victor from vanquish'd issues at the last,
And overthrower from being overthrown.
Well hast thou done; for all the stream is freed,
And thou hast wreak'd his justice on his foes,
And when reviled, hast answer'd graciously,
And makest merry, when overthrown.   Prince,
　　Knight,
Hail, Knight and Prince, and of our Table Round!'

　And then when turning to Lynette he told
The tale of Gareth, petulantly she said,
'Ay well—ay well—for worse than being fool'd
Of others, is to fool one's self. A cave,
Sir Lancelot, is hard by, with meats and drinks
And forage for the horse, and flint for fire.
But all about it flies a honeysuckle.
Seek, till we find.' And when they sought and
　　found,
Sir Gareth drank and ate, and all his life
Past into sleep; on whom the maiden gazed.
'Sound sleep be thine! sound cause to sleep hast
　　thou.
O Lancelot, Lancelot'—and she clapt her hands—
'Full merry am I to find my goodly knave
Is knight and noble. See now, sworn have I,
Else yon black felon had not let me pass,
To bring thee back to do the battle with him.
Thus an thou goest, he will fight thee first;
Who doubts thee victor? so will my knight-knave
Miss the full flower of this accomplishment.'

　Said Lancelot, 'Peradventure he, ye name,
May know my shield. Let Gareth, an he will,

Change his for mine, and take my charger, fresh,
Not to be spurr'd, loving the battle as well
As he that rides him.' 'Lancelot-like,' she said,
'Courteous in this, Lord Lancelot, as in all.'

And Gareth, wakening, fiercely clutch'd the
    shield;
'Ramp ye lance-splintering lions, on whom all
    spears
Are rotten sticks! ye seem agape to roar!
Yea, ramp and roar at leaving of your lord!—
Care not, good beasts, so well I care for you.
O noble Lancelot, from my hold on these
Streams virtue—fire—thro' one that will not shame
Even the shadow of Lancelot under shield.
Hence: let us go.'

    .   .   .   .   .   .

                    Silent the silent field
They traversed. . . . .
Suddenly she that rode upon his left
Clung to the shield that Lancelot lent him, crying,
'Yield, yield him this again: 'tis he must fight:
Miracles ye cannot: here is glory enow
In having flung the three: I see thee maim'd,
Mangled: I swear thou canst not fling the fourth.'

    .   .   .   .

    Then for a space, and under cloud that grew
To thunder-gloom palling all stars, they rode
In converse till she made her palfrey halt,
Lifted an arm, and softly whisper'd, 'There.'
And all the three were silent, seeing, pitch'd
Beside the Castle Perilous on flat field,
A huge pavilion like a mountain peak

Sunder the glooming crimson on the marge,
Black, with black banner, and a long black horn
Beside it hanging; which Sir Gareth graspt,
And so, before the two could hinder him,
Sent all his heart and breath thro' all the horn.
Echo'd the wall; a light twinkled; anon
Came lights and lights, and once again he blew;
Whereon were hollow tramplings up and down
And muffled voices heard, and shadows past;
Till high above him, circled with her maids,
The Lady Lyonors at a window stood,
Beautiful among lights, and waving to him
White hands, and courtesy; but when the Prince
Three times had blown—after long hush—at last—
The huge pavilion slowly yielded up,
Thro' those black foldings, that which housed there-
    in.
High on a nightblack horse, in nightblack arms,
With white breast-bone, and barren ribs of Death,
And crown'd with fleshless laughter — some ten
    steps—
In the half light—thro' the dim dawn—advanced
The monster, and then paused, and spake no word.

    But Gareth spake and all indignantly,
'Fool, for thou hast, men say, the strength of ten,
Canst thou not trust the limbs thy God hath given,
But must, to make the terror of thee more,
Trick thyself out in ghastly imageries
Of that which Life hath done with, and the clod,
Less dull than thou, will hide with mantling flowers
As if for pity?' But he spake no word;
Which set the horror higher: a maiden swoon'd;

THE SPEAKING VOICE

The Lady Lyonors wrung her hands and wept,
As doom'd to be the bride of Night and Death;
Sir Gareth's head prickled beneath his helm;
And ev'n Sir Lancelot thro' his warm blood felt
Ice strike, and all that mark'd him were aghast.

At once Sir Lancelot's charger fiercely neigh'd—
At once the black horse bounded forward with him.
Then those that did not blink the terror, saw
That Death was cast to ground, and slowly rose.
But with one stroke Sir Gareth split the skull.
Half fell to right and half to left and lay.
Then with a stronger buffet he clove the helm
As thoroughly as the skull; and out from this
Issued the bright face of a blooming boy
Fresh as a flower new-born, and crying, 'Knight,
Slay me not: my three brethren bade me do it,
To make a horror all about the house,
And stay the world from Lady Lyonors.
They never dream'd the passes would be past.'
Answer'd Sir Gareth graciously to one
Not many a moon his younger, 'My fair child,
What madness made thee challenge the chief knight
Of Arthur's hall?' 'Fair Sir, they bade me do it.
They hate the King, and Lancelot, the King's
        friend,
They hoped to slay him somewhere on the stream,
They never dream'd the passes could be past.'

Then sprang the happier day from under-
        ground;
And Lady Lyonors and her house, with dance
And revel and song, made merry over Death,

EPIC POETRY

As being after all their foolish fears
And horrors only proven a blooming boy.
So large mirth lived and Gareth won the quest.

And he that told the tale in older times
Says that Sir Gareth wedded Lyonors,
But he that told it later says Lynette."
                                    —ALFRED TENNYSON.

VIII

THE DRAMATIC MONOLOGUE AND THE PLAY

OUR study in the vocal interpretation of literary forms finally reaches the play. The natural approach to the play is through the dramatic monologue. Indeed the play, when presented by one person, becomes a dramatic monologue. The dictionary in defining the monologue authorizes three forms: (1) when the actor tells a continuous story in which he is the chief character, referring to the others as absent; (2) when he assumes the voice or manner of several characters successively; (3) more recently, when he implies that the others are present, leading the audience to imagine what they say by his replies. Browning created this more recent form, which is the most vital of the three. I have chosen for your study of the monologue examples from Browning alone. To interpret effectively any one of the Browning monologues will call into play every element of power in voice and expression which you have gained in your study of previous forms. You must think vividly, feel intelligently; realize and suggest an atmosphere; sustain a situation; and keep the beauty of the poetic form. And you must do all this *in the person of another*. The new demand which the monologue makes is impersonation. Let us see just what we mean by impersonation. It is the art of identifying one's self with the character to be portrayed. It is the art of losing one's self in the character and the situation the dramatist has created. This means that the spirit of the character must take possession of the impersonator, and inform his every thought and feeling and so his every motion and tone. Remember, it is the *spirit* of the character that must determine the nature of the tone and gesture. The great danger in entering upon the study of impersonation lies in emphasizing the outward manifestation instead of the inward spirit of the character to be portrayed. If you really sense the soul, mind, heart quality of the character you are to present, and have made your voice and body free agents for the manifestation of those qualities, your impersonation will be convincing. If the spirit of the Patriot or Andrea del Sarto or Fra Lippo Lippi or Pompilia or Caponsacchi or Guido obsesses you, the outward manifestation will take care of itself—always provided your instruments are responsive. Don't begin with the outward manifestation. Don't say I think this man would frown a great deal, or fold his arms over his breast, or use an eye-glass, or strut, or stoop, or do any one of a hundred things which, if repeated a half-dozen times during an impersonation, may become a mannerism and get between the audience and the spirit of the character. When you are studying a character for the purpose of impersonation determine first to what type it belongs. Then study that type, wherever you are. Daily life becomes your teacher and studio. When you enter upon this art there are no longer dull moments in railroad stations or trains, in shops or in the social whirl. Everywhere and al- ways you are the student seeking to know and understand types of people better, that you may use your knowledge in presenting to an audience an individual. When you have caught the spirit of the individual you must realize the situation out of which this particular individual speaks.

Let us make a special study of the "Tale" (Browning's epilogue to "The Two Poets of Croisic"). It is perhaps the most exquisite of the poet's creations in this field. The situation reveals a young girl recalling to her poet lover an old Greek tale he had once told her. There is a suggestion from some critics that Browning has drawn his wife in this portrait, and through it pays his tribute to her. This immediately affords us a clue to the type of character to which the speaker belongs. We cannot hope (nor do we wish) to *impersonate Mrs. Browning*, but a knowledge of Mrs. Browning and her relation to *her* poet lover, gained through a study of her *Letters and Sonnets*, will lead us more quickly to a comprehension of the speaker and situation in the "Tale."

Obsessed by the spirit of the character and fully realizing the situation our next step is, *in imagination*, to set the stage. This is an important point in presenting a monologue. The impersonator must have a clear idea of his position on his imaginary stage relative to his imaginary interlocutor. But he must remember that *imaginary* stage-setting admits of only delicately suggestive use. This is true of the handling of a monologue at every point. It must be suggestive. The *actor* carries to *completion* the action which the monologuist *suggests*. The art of interpreting a monologue depends upon the discrimination of the impersonator in drawing his line between suggestion and actualization in gesture. The business of the monologuist is to make an appeal to the imagination of the audience so vivid that the imagination of the audience can actualize the suggestion. And the illusion is complete. What are the relative positions of the girl and her lover in the "Tale"? There is nothing in the lines to make our choice arbitrary. It is only important that we determine a relation and keep it consistently throughout the reading. Here is a possible "setting." They are in the poet's study; he is working at his desk; she is sitting in a great chair before the fire, a book in her hand, which she does not read; she is gazing into the flames. She begins dreamily, more to herself than to him — "What a pretty tale you told me." At what point does her tone lose its reflective quality and become more personal? Where does she turn to him? How do we know that he leaves his chair and comes over to sit on the arm of her chair? What calls him to her? What two qualities of feeling run through her mood and determine the color of her tone and the character of her movements. If your study of Mrs. Browning has been intelligent, this interplay of the whimsical and serious in her nature cannot have escaped you, and it will illumine now your impersonation of this girl. It is the secret of the peculiar charm of this creation. The story she tells is an old and well-known one.

THE SPEAKING VOICE

It is the manner of the telling through which we come in touch with an exquisite woman's soul that holds us spellbound. Unless the interpreter catches this secret and reveals it to his audience, he will miss the distinctive feature of the monologue and reduce it to a narrative poem.

A TALE

I

" What a pretty tale you told me
    Once upon a time
   —Said you found it somewhere (scold me!)
    Was it prose or was it rhyme,
Greek or Latin?   Greek, you said,
While your shoulder propped my head.

II

Anyhow there's no forgetting
    This much if no more,
That a poet (pray, no petting!)
    Yes, a bard, sir, famed of yore,
Went where such like used to go,
Singing for a prize, you know.

III

Well, he had to sing, nor merely
  Sing but play the lyre;
Playing was important clearly
  Quite as singing: I desire,
Sir, you keep the fact in mind
For a purpose that's behind.

IV

There stood he, while deep attention
  Held the judges round,
—Judges able, I should mention,
  To detect the slightest sound
Sung or played amiss: such ears
Had old judges, it appears!

V

None the less he sang out boldly,
  Played in time and tune,
Till the judges, weighing coldly
  Each note's worth, seemed, late or soon,
Sure to smile 'In vain one tries
Picking faults out: take the prize!'

VI

When, a mischief! Were they seven
  Strings the lyre possessed?
Oh, and afterward eleven,
  Thank you! Well, sir—who had guessed
Such ill luck in store?—it happed
One of those same seven strings snapped.

THE SPEAKING VOICE

VII

All was lost, then! No! a cricket
  (What 'cicada'? Pooh!)
—Some mad thing that left its thicket
  For mere love of music—flew
With its little heart on fire,
Lighted on the crippled lyre.

VIII

So that when (Ah, joy!) our singer
  For his truant string
Feels with disconcerted finger,
  What does cricket else but fling
Fiery heart forth, sound the note
Wanted by the throbbing throat?

IX

Ay and, ever to the ending,
  Cricket chirps at need,
Executes the hands intending,
  Promptly, perfectly,—indeed
Saves the singer from defeat
With her chirrup low and sweet.

X

Till, at ending, all the judges
  Cry with one assent
'Take the prize—a prize who grudges
  Such a voice and instrument?
Why, we took your lyre for harp,
So it shrilled us forth F sharp!'

XI

Did the conqueror spurn the creature,
  Once its service done?
That's no such uncommon feature
  In the case when Music's son
Finds his Lotte's power too spent
For aiding soul-development.

XII

No! This other, on returning
  Homeward, prize in hand,
Satisfied his bosom's yearning:
  (Sir, I hope you understand!)
—Said 'Some record there must be
Of this cricket's help to me!'

XIII

So, he made himself a statue:
  Marble stood, life-size;
On the lyre, he pointed at you,
  Perched his partner in the prize;
Never more apart you found
Her, he throned, from him, she crowned.

XIV

That's the tale: its application?
  Somebody I know
Hopes one day for reputation
  Thro' his poetry that's—oh,
All so learned and so wise
And deserving of a prize!

211

XV

If he gains one, will some ticket,
  When his statue's built,
Tell the gazer ' 'Twas a cricket
  Helped my crippled lyre, whose lilt
Sweet and low, when strength usurped
Softness' place i' the scale, she chirped?

XVI

'For as victory was nighest,
  While I sang and played—
With my lyre at lowest, highest,
  Right alike,—one string that made
"Love" sound soft was snapt in twain,
Never to be heard again,—

XVII

'Had not a kind cricket fluttered,
  Perched upon the place
Vacant left, and duly uttered
  "Love, Love, Love," whene'er the bass
Asked the treble to atone
For its somewhat sombre drone.'

XVIII

But you don't know music! Wherefore
  Keep on casting pearls
To a—poet? All I care for
  Is—to tell him that a girl's
'Love' comes aptly in when gruff
Grows his singing. (There, enough!)"

212

DRAMATIC MONOLOGUE AND PLAY

INCIDENT OF THE FRENCH CAMP

I

" You know, we French stormed Ratisbon:
    A mile or so away,
On a little mound, Napoleon
    Stood on our storming-day;
With neck out-thrust, you fancy how,
    Legs wide, arms locked behind,
As if to balance the prone brow
    Oppressive with its mind.

II

Just as perhaps he mused 'My plans
    That soar, to earth may fall,
Let once my army-leader Lannes
    Waver at yonder wall,'—
Out 'twixt the battery smokes there flew
    A rider, bound on bound
Full-galloping; nor bridle drew
    Until he reached the mound.

III

Then off there flung in smiling joy,
    And held himself erect
By just his horse's mane, a boy:
    You hardly could suspect—
(So tight he kept his lips compressed,
    Scarce any blood came through)
You looked twice ere you saw his breast
    Was all but shot in two.

IV

'Well,' cried he, 'Emperor, by God's grace
  We've got you Ratisbon!
The Marshal's in the market-place,
  And you'll be there anon
To see your flag-bird flap his vans
  Where I, to heart's desire,
Perched him!' The chief's eye flashed; his plans
  Soared up again like fire.

V

The chief's eye flashed; but presently
  Softened itself, as sheathes
A film the mother-eagle's eye
  When her bruised eaglet breathes;
'You're wounded!' 'Nay,' the soldier's pride
  Touched to the quick, he said:
'I'm killed, Sire!' And his chief beside,
  Smiling the boy fell dead."

MY LAST DUCHESS

FERRARA

"That's my last Duchess painted on the wall,
Looking as if she were alive. I call
That piece a wonder, now: Frà Pandolf's hands
Worked busily a day, and there she stands.
Will 't please you sit and look at her? I said
'Frà Pandolf' by design; for never read

Strangers like you that pictured countenance,
The depth and passion of its earnest glance,
But to myself they turned (since none puts by
The curtain I have drawn for you, but I)
And seemed as they would ask me, if they durst,
How such a glance came there; so, not the first
Are you to turn and ask thus. Sir, 'twas not
Her husband's presence only, called that spot
Of joy into the Duchess' cheek: perhaps
Frà Pandolf chanced to·say 'Her mantle laps
Over my lady's wrist too much,' or 'Paint
Must never hope to reproduce the faint
Half-flush that dies along her throat': such stuff
Was courtesy, she thought, and cause enough
For calling up that spot of joy. She had
A heart—how shall I say?—too soon made glad,
Too easily impressed; she liked whate'er
She looked on, and her looks went everywhere.
Sir, 'twas all one! My favor at her breast,
The dropping of the daylight in the West,
The bough of cherries some officious fool
Broke in the orchard for her, the white mule
She rode with round the terrace—all and each
Would draw from her alike the approving speech,
Or blush, at least. She thanked men, —good!
    but thanked
Somehow—I know not how—as if she ranked
My gift of a nine-hundred-years-old name
With anybody's gift. Who'd stoop to blame
This sort of trifling? Even had you skill
In speech—(which I have not)—to make your will
Quite clear to such an one, and say, 'Just this
Or that in you disgusts me; here you miss,

Or there exceed the mark'—and if she let
Herself be lessoned so, nor plainly set
Her wits to yours, forsooth, and made excuse,
—E'en then would be some stooping; and I
    choose
Never to stoop. Oh sir, she smiled, no doubt,
Whene'er I passed her; but who passed without
Much the same smile? This grew; I gave com-
    mands;
Then all smiles stopped together. There she
    stands
As if alive. Will 't please you rise? We'll meet
The company below, then. I repeat,
The Count your master's known munificence
Is ample warrant that no just pretence
Of mine for dowry will be disallowed;
Though his fair daughter's self, as I avowed
At starting, is my object. Nay, we'll go
Together down, sir. Notice Neptune, though,
Taming a sea-horse, thought a rarity,
Which Claus of Innsbruck cast in bronze for me!"
                —ROBERT BROWNING.

Our last form for interpretative vocal study
is the play. We shall discover that the presentation of the play makes the same demands upon the interpreter as the monologue
with the new element of "transition." We
are still studying the monologue, because we
are to read not act the play. It is still sug-

gestive not actualized impersonation. But instead of one character to suggestively set forth we have two, three, a dozen to present. The transition from character to character becomes our one new problem. As we have said before, in making the transition from character to character, voice, mind, and body must be so volatile that the action of the play shall not be interrupted. I know of no better way to enter upon the study of a play for reading (or acting) than to treat each chararacter as the speaker in a monologue of the Browning type. The danger in transition from character to character centres in the instant's pause when one speaker yields to another. The unskilful reader loses both characters at this point and becomes conscious of himself; the action of the play stops; and the illusion of scene and situation is lost. The great reader of the play (in that " instant's pause "), as he utters the last word of one character, becomes the interlocutor listening to the words which he as the other character has just uttered. In that instant he must show the effect of the speech he has just uttered upon the character he has just become. *Which is the greater art : to read a play, or to act in it ?*

Use for your study of the play the Shakespearian drama. Begin with scenes from "As You Like It" and "The Merchant of Venice."

9 781437 384802